Terence Rattigan

THE DEEP
BLUE SEA

With introductions by
Sean O'Connor *and* Dan Rebellato

T0284719

NICK HERN BOOKS

London

www.nickhernbooks.co.uk

A Nick Hern Book

This film tie-in edition of *The Deep Blue Sea* first published in Great Britain in 2011 as a paperback original by Nick Hern Books Limited, 14 Larden Road, London W3 7ST

First published by Nick Hern Books in 1999, by arrangement with Methuen Drama. *The Deep Blue Sea* was included in Volume Two of *The Collected Plays of Terence Rattigan* published in 1953 by Hamish Hamilton

Cover image of Rachel Weisz and Tom Hiddleston in the 2011 film of *The Deep Blue Sea*, courtesy of Artificial Eye
Cover design: Ned Hoste, 2H

Typeset by Nick Hern Books, London
Printed in the UK by Mimeo Ltd, Huntingdon, Cambs PE29 6XX

A CIP catalogue record for this book is available from the British Library

ISBN 978 1 84842 234 6

From Stage to Screen: Terence Rattigan, Terence Davies and *The Deep Blue Sea*

Sean O'Connor
Producer, The Deep Blue Sea

In the mid-1990s, I was researching a book about Oscar Wilde, Somerset Maugham, Noël Coward and Terence Rattigan – playwrights who articulated a subversive agenda at the heart of that apparently most conventional of forms, the 'well-made play'. Here were a whole series of plays, deeply cynical about the institution of marriage and intent on exposing the fragility of family life – an extraordinarily radical agenda at the heart of West End popular theatre.

In my research, I interviewed the original director of *The Deep Blue Sea*, Frith Banbury – then in his eighties – who had been a friend of Rattigan's at Oxford. He had also known Rattigan's lover, Kenneth Morgan, appearing with him in Rattigan's short-lived anti-Nazi play, *Follow My Leader*, in 1940. It was Morgan's later suicide over another man that inspired Rattigan to write *The Deep Blue Sea*, exploring as it did, one of Rattigan's defining themes – the differing and irreconcilable definition each of us has of the notion of Love.

I became great friends with Frith and he'd often talk about the playwrights he had worked with (Rattigan, Robert Bolt, Wynyard Browne, Rodney Ackland, N.C. Hunter) and the actors he had directed – a roll call of the celebrated names of the mid-twentieth-century British theatre – Ralph Richardson, Edith Evans, Celia Johnson, Paul Scofield, Wendy Hiller, Michael Redgrave, Deborah Kerr and, of course, Peggy Ashcroft, whom Frith had immediately wanted to play Hester when he first read *The Deep Blue Sea* (Rattigan wanted his friend, Margaret Leighton; Frith thought her *far* too glamorous). Frith was fascinating about the genesis and rehearsal process of *The Deep*

Blue Sea: the suburban but sensual Peggy Ashcroft struggling with Hester's extraordinary physical need; Rattigan struggling to articulate a satisfactory ending to the play. When he died in 2008, I wondered if there might be a way of celebrating Frith's achievements, given that, as a man very much of the theatre, there was little that survived of his celebrated productions other than some long-forgotten reviews and black-and-white production photographs by Angus McBean.

I approached Rattigan's agent, Alan Brodie, to ask if the film rights to *The Deep Blue Sea* might be available. The play had been filmed before in 1955 to poor reviews – though Kenneth More won the award for Best Actor at that year's Venice Film Festival. Despite the talents of Vivien Leigh – in her first screen role since her Oscar-winning Blanche Dubois in 1951 – the film is flawed. The action takes place in a huge, almost ambassadorial residence on Chelsea Embankment, rather than Rattigan's shabby Ladbroke Grove. Rattigan's screenplay opens out the play dramatically, and we even get to see Freddie and Hester flirting on the ski slopes of San Moritz – Kenneth More sporting a none-too-sexy bobble hat. Vivien Leigh as Hester is icily haughty in Lady Olivier mode, with none of the vulnerability that helped Peggy Ashcroft make the play a West End hit.

Surprisingly, for such a successful and well-known play, the film didn't engage the public's imagination. Still unavailable today on DVD and hardly ever broadcast on television, the film has become, effectively, lost. Alan was happy to say that the rights were available and wouldn't it be a wonderful idea to attempt a new screen version in time for the centenary of Rattigan's birth in 2011? This seemed a very swift trajectory (this being 2009), but we felt it was worth giving a shot.

The first – and only – director for the film that came to my mind was Terence Davies. I had seen – and loved – *Distant Voices, Still Lives* when it first came out in 1988: the graceful tracking shots, the use of popular and classical music, the focus on women *in extremis*. Crucially, Terence Davies is a poet. He's deeply moved by the internal rhythms of poetry and music. It's not surprising that his favourite work of art is T. S. Eliot's *Four Quartets*.

Terence hadn't made a feature film since *The House of Mirth* in 2000, and I wasn't even sure if he was interested in making films any more, but I tracked him down and we arranged to meet in a restaurant. We didn't talk about the play very much, but we did talk about the films that we liked: *Brief Encounter*, *Now Voyager*, *All That Heaven Allows*; and the leading actresses that flourished in the 1940s and '50s: Googie Withers, Celia Johnson, Margaret Lockwood, Jean Kent, Bette Davis. It's probably in this conversation that we defined what the film we'd like to make could be: Terence Davies's unique version of a 1940s 'woman's picture' – full of his love and memory of the films of his youth.

At the end of lunch, Terence slipped a manuscript across the table and said, in his deep, hushed tones, 'I've written the first five pages of the screenplay. Would you like me to read it to you?' On the basis of a few emails – and no commitment – he had already started writing. With the restaurant nearly empty, Terence read the opening sequence of the film, speaking out the stage directions, stopping to dramatise camera movements and even hissing the sound of the gas; I was completely hooked.

Later, Terence was to tell me, 'If I can see the opening scenes, then I know it's going to be okay.' And indeed, this was to prove true throughout the development and shooting of the film: Terence's reactions are instinctive, personal, sometimes apparently illogical – but always aiming for a pared-down simplicity – a sense of truth.

As I left the restaurant, Terence stopped me and said that he had chosen the music he would like to use: the Second Movement of Samuel Barber's Violin Concerto. 'It's *knockout*,' he said, again with his infectious enthusiasm. True enough, I bought a copy of the Concerto on the way home, and played it. The piece was new to me – and a revelation in the context of Rattigan's play. What Terence had understood is the great depths of emotion that lie at the heart of *The Deep Blue Sea* – despite the period setting, there's a timeless, classical stature to Hester's dark night of the soul – and it was this that Terence was keen to reveal.

Over the next year, Terence worked on the text of the screenplay – sometimes submitting versions that had barely changed, sometimes offering radically different drafts. But as he did so, it was clear that he was carefully working towards his own vision of what the film might be – what the core of the story was – and most importantly, what the meaning of the film was specifically for *him*. And at every point, Alan Brodie and the Rattigan Estate were fully behind Terence's vision – encouraging, emboldening. They wanted him to forget that it was a celebrated classic of the theatre and to be more radical with the text, to make it a piece of cinema – in effect, to make it more like a Terence Davies film. And it's this collusion between the two Terences – Terence Rattigan, the master of theatre, and Terence Davies, the cinematic poet – that has resulted in this new screen version of *The Deep Blue Sea*.

Two films that became crucial in the evolution of the screenplay were Robert Hamer's *It Always Rains On Sunday* and Noël Coward/David Lean's *Brief Encounter*. In *It Always Rains on Sunday*, an ordinary woman (Googie Withers) in an ordinary street has an extraordinary day as an ex-lover – and now escaped convict – comes back into her life. The whole film, like the play version of *The Deep Blue Sea*, takes place over a day and is framed by the East End street where Withers' character lives – a structure that Terence Davies delighted in referring to in the opening and closing shots of *The Deep Blue Sea*. And in Withers' relationship with the convict (John McCallum) there is an extraordinary sensuality – very unusual for British films of the period. It's this earthy human need that Terence was keen to bring to Hester's story.

In *Brief Encounter*, the whole story is told from the point of view of Celia Johnson's character, everything is filtered through her memory. For Terence Davies, for whom memory and the passage of time are hugely rich, this was a breakthrough. For a character like Hester who might seem rather unsympathetic to a twenty-first-century audience, this was a way of getting inside her consciousness, guiding the audience through her life and showing them why she ultimately feels compelled to take her own life. The music, too, was woven throughout the screenplay right from the first draft, echoing the use of Rachmaninov in *Brief Encounter* – the music articulating the protagonist's emotional turmoil.

Terence's screenplay gets to the anguished heart of Rattigan's original dialogue, but is generally much sparer and simpler. The scenes with supporting characters are cut back to concentrate more fully on the central dilemma. We also see Hester at home with her husband, visiting his mother in her country house, and being driven to dinner in a Rolls-Royce. All of these moments allow the audience to witness the very privileged life that Hester has given up in order to live with Freddie. Having seen the comparatively luxurious life she has forfeited – and the shabbiness of the bedsit that she now lives in – we realise the height she has fallen from, and into what dire circumstances: a cultured woman reduced to pub crawls, ugly rows and desperate love-making.

Terence's cinematic responses to the story are fascinating. He opens the story with Hester deciding to kill herself on Sunday night, rather than (as in the play) the morning after. This means that we have actually seen Hester preparing for suicide: the shillings in the meter, the towel under the door. As she also does so in Act Three when Freddie has put the phone down on her, how could we prevent one of the most dramatic moments in the film (another suicide attempt) from being repetitive? The answer was in Rattigan's various drafts of the play in the British Library. In one draft, Rattigan has Hester cutting her wrists on a broken glass in Act Three. So maybe, we thought, we should be looking for an alternative to the gas fire altogether? And, as we had the option of going anywhere to shoot it, surely it should be a uniquely London setting? Perhaps Hester should consider drowning herself in the Thames (it is called *The Deep Blue Sea*, after all)?

But what could be more 'London' than a Tube station? And what better homage to *Brief Encounter* than to have the heroine threaten to throw herself under a train? Consequently, Hester's second suicide attempt is now one of the crux moments of the story and also – a single tracking shot – one of the definitive 'Terence Davies' moments of the film.

One of the great revelations of opening out the action of the play is how the context of the story – the dark days of austerity Britain in a landscape scarred by bombsites, a populace exhausted by rationing and a nation brought its knees by bankruptcy – impacts on the characters. As Michael Billington has noted, the triangle of relationships at the heart of the story hints at the dilemmas of the entire British nation in the early post-war period. Hester, like many women, has been liberated from the mores and conventions of the pre-war period, but having embraced the path of danger and passion, is now unsure how to use her freedom. Freddie, her lover, is in a state of stasis, stuck in the period of his finest hour in 1940 and now directionless and empty, comforted only by drink and nostalgia. Collyer, Hester's husband, is the representative of an outmoded, patrician class unable to give his wife either children or sex. Together they represent a nation, bereft of status and Empire, crawling out of the wreckage of the war into the light, but unsure of the future.

Rattigan's beautifully structured play starts in the morning and continues into the night. As Terence developed the screenplay, he chose for the film to open at night – the darkest moment of Hester's life – but he was very keen to end the film the next morning. In essence, this seemingly small idea gave everybody working on the film a great insight into Terence's vision for it. Hester was to go through a period of metaphorical darkness (effectively, lost in the deep blue sea) but would end her story bathed in light. After Freddie leaves her for ever, Hester lights the gas fire, opens the curtains and faces the day. Despite the surrounding bombsites, the camera and the uplifting swell of Barber's music suggest some sort of future for Hester, with the dome of St Paul's – that symbol of defiant survival – just visible on the horizon. No rainbows and cloudless skies in the distance by any means, but it's an ending expressing qualified hope for Hester: she will be poorer perhaps, and maybe lonely, but at least she'll have a future on her own terms.

In 2012, *The Deep Blue Sea* will be sixty years old – one of the very few plays of the 1950s that still feel relevant and true. It's a testament to Rattigan's vision and artistry that the play has survived into the twenty-first century and now seems to have joined that handful of plays that are indisputably regarded as 'classics'.

I think Rattigan – and Frith – would have been very proud of that.

UK Film Council and Film4, in association with Protagonist
Pictures, Lip Sync Productions and Artificial Eye present
A Camberwell/Fly Film Production

The Deep Blue Sea
By Terence Rattigan

Cast (*in order of appearance*)

MRS ELTON	Ann Mitchell
PHILIP WELCH	Jolyon Coy
MR MILLER	Karl Johnson
HESTER COLLYER	Rachel Weisz
SIR WILLIAM COLLYER	Simon Russell Beale
FREDDIE PAGE	Tom Hiddleston
JACKIE JACKSON	Harry Hadden-Paton
LIZ JACKSON	Sarah Kants
HESTER'S FATHER	Oliver Ford Davies
COLLYER'S MOTHER	Barbara Jefford
EDE & RAVENSCROFT ASSISTANT	Mark Tandy
SINGING MAN IN TUBE	Stuart McLoughlin
MR ELTON	Nicholas Amer

Adapter and Director	Terence Davies
Producers	Sean O'Connor
	Kate Ogborn
Executive Producers	Katherine Butler
	Lisa Marie Russo
	Peter Hampden
	Norman Merry
Director of Photography	Florian Hoffmeister

x

Production Designer	James Merifield
Editor	David Charap
Casting Director	Jane Arnell
Costume Designer	Ruth Myers
Hair and Make-Up Designer	Lizzie Yianni Georgiou
Sound Designer	Tim Barker
Line Producer	Eliza Mellor

Made with the support of the UK Film Council's Development
and Film Funds

An Artificial Eye Release
artificial-eye.com

Terence Rattigan (1911–1977)

Dan Rebellato

Terence Rattigan stood on the steps of the Royal Court Theatre, on 8 May 1956, after the opening night of John Osborne's *Look Back in Anger*. Asked by a reporter what he thought of the play, he replied, with an uncharacteristic lack of discretion, that it should have been retitled 'Look how unlike Terence Rattigan I'm being.'[1] And he was right. The great shifts in British theatre, marked by Osborne's famous premiere, ushered in kinds of playwriting which were specifically unlike Rattigan's work. The pre-eminence of playwriting as a formal craft, the subtle tracing of the emotional lives of the middle classes – those techniques which Rattigan so perfected – fell dramatically out of favour, creating a veil of prejudice through which his work even now struggles to be seen.

Terence Mervyn Rattigan was born on 10 June 1911, a wet Saturday a few days before George V's coronation. His father, Frank, was in the diplomatic corps and Terry's parents were often posted abroad, leaving him to be raised by his paternal grandmother. Frank Rattigan was a geographically and emotionally distant man, who pursued a string of little-disguised affairs throughout his marriage. Rattigan would later draw on these memories when he created Mark St Neots, the bourgeois Casanova of *Who is Sylvia?* Rattigan was much closer to his mother, Vera Rattigan, and they remained close friends until her death in 1971.

Rattigan's parents were not great theatregoers, but Frank Rattigan's brother had married a Gaiety Girl, causing a minor family uproar, and an apocryphal story suggests that the 'indulgent aunt' reported as taking the young Rattigan to the theatre may have been this scandalous relation.[2] And when, in the summer of 1922, his family went to stay in the country cottage of the drama critic Hubert Griffiths, Rattigan avidly worked through his extensive library of playscripts. Terry went to Harrow in 1925, and there maintained both his somewhat illicit theatregoing habit and his insatiable reading, reputedly devouring every play in the school library. Apart from contemporary authors like Galsworthy, Shaw and Barrie, he also read the plays of Chekhov, a writer whose crucial influence he often acknowledged.[3]

His early attempts at writing, while giving little sign of his later sophistication, do indicate his ability to absorb and reproduce his own theatrical experiences. There was a ten-minute melodrama about the Borgias entitled *The Parchment*, on the cover of which the author recommends with admirable conviction that a suitable cast for this work might comprise 'Godfrey Tearle, Gladys Cooper, Marie Tempest, Matheson Lang, Isobel Elsom, Henry Ainley… [and] Noël Coward'.[4] At Harrow, when one of his teachers demanded a French playlet for a composition exercise, Rattigan, undaunted by his linguistic shortcomings, produced a full-throated tragedy of deception, passion and revenge which included the immortal curtain line: 'COMTESSE. (*Souffrant terriblement.*) Non! non! non! Ah non! Mon Dieu, non!'[5] His teacher's now famous response was 'French execrable: theatre sense first class'.[6] A year later, aged fifteen, he wrote *The Pure in Heart,* a rather more substantial play showing a family being pulled apart by a son's crime and the father's desire to maintain his reputation. Rattigan's ambitions were plainly indicated on the title pages, each of which announced the author to be 'the famous playwrite and author T. M. Rattigan.'[7]

Frank Rattigan was less than keen on having a 'playwrite' for a son and was greatly relieved when in 1930, paving the way for a life as a diplomat, Rattigan gained a scholarship to read History at Trinity, Oxford. But Rattigan's interests were entirely elsewhere. A burgeoning political conscience that had led him to oppose the compulsory Officer Training Corps parades at Harrow saw him voice pacifist and socialist arguments at college, even supporting the controversial Oxford Union motion 'This House will in no circumstances fight for its King and Country' in February 1933. The rise of Hitler (which he briefly saw close at hand when he spent some weeks in the Black Forest in July 1933) and the outbreak of the Spanish Civil War saw his radical leanings deepen and intensify. Rattigan never lost his political compassion. After the war he drifted towards the Liberal Party, but he always insisted that he had never voted Conservative, despite the later conception of him as a Tory playwright of the establishment.[8]

Away from the troubled atmosphere of his family, Rattigan began to gain in confidence as the contours of his ambitions and his identity moved more sharply into focus. He soon took advantage of the university's theatrical facilities and traditions. He joined the Oxford Union Dramatic Society (OUDS), where contemporaries included Giles Playfair, George Devine, Peter Glenville, Angus Wilson and Frith Banbury. Each year, OUDS ran a one-act play competition and in Autumn 1931 Rattigan submitted one. Unusually, it seems that this was a highly experimental effort, somewhat like Konstantin's piece in *The Seagull*. George Devine, the OUDS president, apparently told the young author, 'Some of it is absolutely smashing, but it goes too far.'[9] Rattigan was instead to make his first mark as a somewhat scornful reviewer for the student newspaper, *Cherwell*, and as a performer in the Smokers (OUDS's private revue club), where he adopted the persona and dress of 'Lady Diana Coutigan', a drag performance which allowed him to discuss leading members of the Society with a barbed camp wit.[10]

That the name of his Smokers persona echoed the contemporary phrase, 'queer as a coot', indicates Rattigan's new-found confidence in his homosexuality. In February 1932, Rattigan played a tiny part in the OUDS production of *Romeo and Juliet*, which was directed by John Gielgud and starred Peggy Ashcroft and Edith Evans (women undergraduates were not admitted to OUDS, and professional actresses were often recruited). Rattigan's failure to deliver his one line correctly raised an increasingly embarrassing laugh every night (an episode which he reuses to great effect in *Harlequinade*). However, out of this production came a friendship with Gielgud and his partner, John Perry. Through them, Rattigan was introduced to theatrical and homosexual circles, where his youthful 'school captain' looks were much admired.

A growing confidence in his sexuality and in his writing led to his first major play. In 1931, he shared rooms with a contemporary of his, Philip Heimann, who was having an affair with Irina Basilevich, a mature student. Rattigan's own feelings for Heimann completed an eternal triangle that formed the basis of the play he co-wrote with Heimann, *First Episode.* This play was accepted for production in Surrey's 'Q' theatre; it was respectfully received and subsequently transferred to the Comedy Theatre in London's West End, though carefully shorn of its homosexual subplot. Despite receiving only £50 from this production (and having put £200 into it), Rattigan immediately dropped out of college to become a full-time writer.

Frank Rattigan was displeased by this move, but made a deal with his son. He would give him an allowance of £200 a year for two years and let him live at home to write; if at the end of that period, he had had no discernible success, he would enter a more secure and respectable profession. With this looming deadline, Rattigan wrote quickly. *Black Forest*, an O'Neill-inspired play based on his experiences in Germany in 1933, is one of the three that have survived. Rather unwillingly, he collaborated with Hector Bolitho on an adaptation of the latter's novel, *Grey Farm*, which received a disastrous New York production in 1940. Another project was an adaptation of *A Tale of Two Cities*, written with Gielgud; this fell through at the last minute when Donald Albery, the play's potential producer, received a complaint from actor-manager John Martin-Harvey who was beginning a farewell tour of his own adaptation, *The Only Way*, which he had been performing for forty-five years. As minor compensation, Albery invited Rattigan to send him any other new scripts. Rattigan sent him a play provisionally titled *Gone Away*, based on his experiences in a French-language summer school in 1931. Albery took out a nine-month option on it, but no production appeared.

By mid-1936, Rattigan was despairing. His father had secured him a job with Warner Brothers as an in-house screenwriter, which was reasonably paid; but Rattigan wanted success in the theatre, and his desk-bound life at Teddington Studios seemed unlikely to advance this ambition. By chance, one of Albery's productions was unexpectedly losing money, and the wisest course of action seemed to be to pull the show and replace it with something cheap. Since *Gone Away* required a relatively small cast and only one set, Albery quickly arranged for a production. Harold French, the play's director, had only one qualm: the title. Rattigan suggested *French Without Tears*, which was immediately adopted.

After an appalling dress rehearsal, no one anticipated the rapturous response of the first-night audience, led by Cicely Courtneidge's infectious laugh. The following morning Kay Hammond, the show's female lead, discovered Rattigan surrounded by the next day's reviews. 'But I don't believe it,' he said. 'Even *The Times* likes it.'[11]

French Without Tears played over 1000 performances in its three-year run and Rattigan was soon earning £100 a week. He moved out of his father's home, wriggled out of his Warner Brothers contract, and dedicated himself to spending the money as soon as it came in. Partly this was an attempt to defer the moment when he had to follow up this enormous success. In the event, both of his next plays were undermined by the outbreak of war.

After the Dance, an altogether more bleak indictment of the Bright Young Things' failure to engage with the iniquities and miseries of contemporary life, opened, in June 1939, to euphoric reviews; but only a month later the European crisis was darkening the national mood and audiences began to dwindle. The play was pulled in August after only sixty performances. *Follow My Leader* was a satirical farce closely based on the rise of Hitler, co-written with an Oxford contemporary, Tony Goldschmidt (writing as Anthony Maurice in case anyone thought he was German). It suffered an alternative fate. Banned from production in 1938, owing to the Foreign Office's belief that 'the production of this play at this time would not be in the best interests of the country',[12] it finally received its premiere in 1940, by which time Rattigan and Goldschmidt's mild satire failed to capture the real fears that the war was unleashing in the country.

Rattigan's insecurity about writing now deepened. An interest in Freud, dating back to his Harrow days, encouraged him to visit a psychiatrist that he had known while at Oxford, Dr Keith Newman. Newman exerted a Svengali-like influence on Rattigan and persuaded the pacifist playwright to join the RAF as a means of curing his writer's block. Oddly, this unorthodox treatment seemed to have some effect; by 1941, Rattigan was writing again. On one dramatic sea crossing, an engine failed, and with everyone forced to jettison all excess baggage and possessions, Rattigan threw the hard covers and blank pages from the notebook containing his new play, stuffing the precious manuscript into his jacket.

Rattigan drew on his RAF experiences to write a new play, *Flare Path*. Bronson Albery and Bill Linnit who had supported *French Without Tears* both turned the play down, believing that the last thing that the public wanted was a play about the war.[13] H. M. Tennent Ltd., led by the elegant Hugh 'Binkie' Beaumont, was the third management offered the script; and in 1942, *Flare Path* opened in London, eventually playing almost 700 performances. Meticulously interweaving the stories of three couples against the backdrop of wartime uncertainty, Rattigan found himself 'commended, if not exactly as a professional playwright, at least as a promising apprentice who had definitely begun to learn the rudiments of his job'.[14] Beaumont, already on the way to becoming the most powerful and successful West End producer of the era, was an influential ally for Rattigan. There is a curious side-story to this production; Dr Keith Newman decided to watch 250 performances of this play and write up the insights that his 'serial attendance' had afforded him. George Bernard Shaw remarked that such playgoing behaviour 'would have driven me mad; and I am not sure that [Newman] came out of it without a slight derangement'. Shaw's caution was wise.[15] In late 1945, Newman went insane and eventually died in a psychiatric hospital.

Meanwhile, Rattigan had achieved two more successes; the witty farce, *While the Sun Shines*, and the more serious, though politically clumsy, *Love in Idleness* (retitled *O Mistress Mine* in America). He had also co-written a number of successful films, including *The Day Will Dawn, Uncensored, The Way to the Stars* and an adaptation of *French Without Tears*. By the end of 1944, Rattigan had three plays running in the West End, a record only beaten by Somerset Maugham's four in 1908.

Love in Idleness was dedicated to Henry 'Chips' Channon, the Tory MP who had become Rattigan's lover. Channon's otherwise gossipy diaries record their meeting very discreetly: 'I dined with Juliet Duff in her little flat... also there, Sibyl Colefax and Master Terence Rattigan, and we sparkled over the Burgundy. I like Rattigan enormously, and feel a new friendship has begun. He has a flat in Albany.'[16] Tom Driberg's rather less discreet account fleshes out the story: Channon's 'seduction of the playwright was almost like the wooing of Danaë by Zeus – every day the playwright found, delivered to his door, a splendid present – a case of champagne, a huge pot of caviar, a Cartier cigarette box in two kinds of gold… In the end, of course, he gave in, saying apologetically to his friends, "How can one *not*?".'[17] It was a very different set in which Rattigan now moved, one that was wealthy and conservative, the very people he had criticised in *After the Dance*. Rattigan did not share the complacency of many of his friends, and his next play revealed a deepening complexity and ambition.

For a long time, Rattigan had nurtured a desire to become respected as a serious writer; the commercial success of *French Without Tears* had, however, sustained the public image of Rattigan as a wealthy, young, light-comedy writer-about-town.[18] With *The Winslow Boy*, which premiered in 1946, Rattigan began to turn this image around. In doing so he entered a new phase as a playwright. As one contemporary critic observed, this play 'put him at once into the class of the serious and distinguished writer'.[19] The play, based on the Archer-Shee case in which a family attempted to sue the Admiralty for a false accusation of theft against their son, featured some of Rattigan's most elegantly crafted and subtle characterisation yet. The famous second curtain, when the barrister Robert Morton subjects Ronnie Winslow to a vicious interrogation before announcing that 'The boy is plainly innocent. I accept the brief', brought a joyous standing ovation on the first night. No less impressive is the subtle handling of the concept of 'justice' and 'rights' through the play of ironies which pits Morton's liberal complacency against Catherine Winslow's feminist convictions.

Two years later, Rattigan's *Playbill*, comprising the one-act plays *The Browning Version* and *Harlequinade*, showed an ever deepening talent. The latter is a witty satire of the kind of touring theatre encouraged by the new Committee for the Encouragement of Music and Arts (CEMA, the immediate forerunner of the Arts Council). But the former's depiction of a failed, repressed Classics teacher evinced an ability to choreograph emotional subtleties on stage that outstripped anything Rattigan had yet demonstrated.

Adventure Story, which in 1949 followed hard on the heels of *Playbill*, was less successful. An attempt to dramatise the emotional dilemmas of Alexander the Great, Rattigan seemed unable to escape the vernacular of his own circle, and the epic scheme of the play sat oddly with Alexander's more prosaic concerns.

Rattigan's response to both the critical bludgeoning of this play and the distinctly lukewarm reception of *Playbill* on Broadway was to write a somewhat extravagant article for the *New Statesman*. 'Concerning the Play of Ideas' was a desire to defend the place of 'character' against those who would insist on the pre-eminence in drama of ideas.[20] The essay is not clear and is couched in such teasing terms that it is at first difficult to see why it should have secured such a fervent response. James Bridie, Benn Levy, Peter Ustinov, Sean O'Casey, Ted Willis, Christopher Fry and finally George Bernard Shaw all weighed in to support or condemn the article. Finally Rattigan replied in slightly more moderate terms to these criticisms insisting (and the first essay reasonably supports this) that he was not calling for the end of ideas in the theatre, but rather for their inflection through character and situation.[21] However, the damage was done (as, two years later, with his 'Aunt Edna', it would again be done). Rattigan was increasingly being seen as the arch-proponent of commercial vacuity.[22]

The play Rattigan had running at the time added weight to his opponents' charge. Originally planned as a dark comedy, *Who is Sylvia?* became a rather more frivolous thing both in the writing and the playing. Rattled by the failure of *Adventure Story*, and superstitiously aware that the new play was opening at the Criterion, where fourteen years before *French Without Tears* had been so successful, Rattigan and everyone involved in the production had steered it towards light farce and obliterated the residual seriousness of the original conceit.

Rattigan had ended his affair with Henry Channon and taken up with Kenneth Morgan, a young actor who had appeared in *Follow My Leader* and the film of *French Without Tears*. However, the relationship had not lasted and Morgan had for a while been seeing someone else. Rattigan's distress was compounded one day in February 1949, when he received a message that Morgan had killed himself. Although horrified, Rattigan soon began to conceive an idea for a play. Initially it was to have concerned a homosexual relationship, but Beaumont, his producer, persuaded him to change the relationship to a heterosexual one.[23] At a time when the Lord Chamberlain refused to allow any plays to be staged that featured homosexuality, such a proposition would have been a commercial impossibility. The result is one of the finest examples of Rattigan's craft. The story of Hester Collyer, trapped in a relationship with a man incapable of returning her love, and her transition from attempted suicide to groping, uncertain self-determination is handled with extraordinary economy, precision and power. The depths of despair and desire that Rattigan plumbs have made *The Deep Blue Sea* one of his most popular and moving pieces.

1953 saw Rattigan's romantic comedy *The Sleeping Prince*, planned as a modest, if belated, contribution to the Coronation festivities. However, the project was hypertrophied by the insistent presence of Laurence Olivier and Vivien Leigh in the cast and the critics were disturbed to see such whimsy from the author of *The Deep Blue Sea.*

Two weeks after its opening, the first two volumes of Rattigan's *Collected Plays* were published. The preface to the second volume introduced one of Rattigan's best-known, and most notorious creations: Aunt Edna. 'Let us invent,' he writes, 'a character, a nice respectable, middle-class, middle-aged, maiden lady, with time on her hands and the money to help her pass it.'[24] Rattigan paints a picture of this eternal theatregoer, whose bewildered disdain for modernism ('Picasso – "those dreadful reds, my dear, and why three noses?"')[25] make up part of the particular challenge of dramatic writing. The intertwined commercial and cultural pressures that the audience brings with it exert considerable force on the playwright's work.

Rattigan's creation brought considerable scorn upon his head. But Rattigan is neither patronising nor genuflecting towards Aunt Edna. The whole essay is aimed at demonstrating the crucial role of the audience in the theatrical experience. Rattigan's own sense of theatre was *learned* as a member of the audience, and he refuses to distance himself from this woman:

'despite my already self-acknowledged creative ambitions I did not in the least feel myself a being apart. If my neighbours gasped with fear for the heroine when she was confronted with a fate worse than death, I gasped with them'.[26] But equally, he sees his job as a writer to engage in a gentle tug-of-war with the audience's expectations: 'although Aunt Edna must never be made mock of, or bored, or befuddled, she must equally not be wooed, or pandered to or cosseted'.[27] The complicated relation between satisfying and surprising this figure may seem contradictory, but as Rattigan notes, 'Aunt Edna herself is indeed a highly contradictory character.'[28]

But Rattigan's argument, as in the 'Play of Ideas' debate before it, was taken to imply an insipid pandering to the unchallenging expectations of his audience. Aunt Edna dogged his career from that moment on and she became such a byword for what theatre should *not* be that in 1960, the Questors Theatre, Ealing, could title a triple-bill of Absurdist plays, 'Not For Aunt Edna'.[29]

Rattigan's next play did help to restore his reputation as a serious dramatist. *Separate Tables* was another double-bill, set in a small Bournemouth hotel. The first play develops Rattigan's familiar themes of sexual longing and humiliation while the second pits a man found guilty of interfering with women in a local cinema against the self-appointed moral jurors in the hotel. The evening was highly acclaimed and the subsequent Broadway production a rare American success.

However, Rattigan's reign as the leading British playwright was about to be brought to an abrupt end. In a car from Stratford to London, early in 1956, Rattigan spent two and a half hours informing his Oxford contemporary George Devine why the new play he had discovered would not work in the theatre. When Devine persisted, Rattigan answered 'Then I know nothing about plays.' To which Devine replied, 'You know everything about plays, but you don't know a fucking thing about *Look Back in Anger.*'[30] Rattigan only barely attended the first night. He and Hugh Beaumont wanted to leave at the interval until the critic T. C. Worsley persuaded them to stay.[31]

The support for the English Stage Company's initiative was soon overwhelming. Osborne's play was acclaimed by the influential critics Kenneth Tynan and Harold Hobson, and the production was revived frequently at the Court, soon standing as the banner under which that disparate band of men (and women), the Angry Young Men, would assemble. Like many of his contemporaries, Rattigan decried the new movements, Beckett and Ionesco's turn from Naturalism, the wild invective of Osborne, the passionate socialism of Wesker, the increasing influence of Brecht. His opposition to them was perhaps intemperate, but he knew what was at stake: 'I may be prejudiced, but I'm pretty sure it won't survive,' he said in 1960, 'I'm prejudiced because if it *does* survive, I know I won't.'[32]

Such was the power and influence of the new movement that Rattigan almost immediately seemed old-fashioned. And from now on, his plays began to receive an almost automatic panning. His first play since *Separate Tables* (1954) was *Variation on a Theme* (1958). But between those dates the critical mood had changed. To make matters worse, there was the widely publicised story that nineteen-year-old Shelagh Delaney had written the successful *A Taste of Honey* in two weeks after having seen *Variation on a Theme* and deciding that she could do better. A more sinister aspect of the response was the increasingly open accusation that Rattigan was dishonestly concealing a covert homosexual play within an apparently heterosexual one. The two champions of Osborne's play, Tynan and Hobson, were joined by Gerard Fay in the *Manchester Guardian* and Alan Brien in the *Spectator* to ask 'Are Things What They Seem?'[33]

When he is not being attacked for smuggling furtively homosexual themes into apparently straight plays, Rattigan is also criticised for lacking the courage to 'come clean' about his sexuality, both in his life and in his writing.[34] But neither of these criticisms really hit the mark. On the one hand, it is rather disingenuous to suggest that Rattigan should have 'come out'. The 1950s were a difficult time for homosexual men. The flight to the Soviet Union of Burgess and Maclean in 1951 sparked off a major witch-hunt against homosexuals, especially those in prominent positions. Cecil Beaton and Benjamin Britten were rumoured to be targets.[35] The police greatly stepped up the investigation and entrapment of homosexuals and prosecutions rose dramatically at the end of the forties, reaching a peak in 1953–4. One of their most infamous arrests for importuning, in October 1953, was that of John Gielgud.[36]

But neither is it quite correct to imply that somehow Rattigan's plays are *really* homosexual. This would be to misunderstand the way that homosexuality figured in the forties and early fifties. Wartime London saw a considerable expansion in the number of pubs and bars where homosexual men (and women) could meet. This network sustained a highly sophisticated system of gestural and dress codes, words and phrases that could be used to indicate one's sexual desires, many of them drawn from theatrical slang. But the illegality of any homosexual activity ensured that these codes could never become *too* explicit, *too* clear. Homosexuality, then, was explored and experienced through a series of semi-hidden, semi-open codes of behaviour; the image of the iceberg, with the greater part of its bulk submerged beneath the surface, was frequently employed.[37] And this image is, of course, one of the metaphors often used to describe Rattigan's own playwriting.

Reaction came in the form of a widespread paranoia about the apparent increase in homosexuality. The fifties saw a major drive to seek out, understand, and often 'cure' homosexuality. The impetus of these investigations was to bring the unspeakable and underground activities of, famously, 'Evil Men' into the open, to make it fully visible. The Wolfenden Report of 1957 was, without doubt, a certain kind of liberalising document in its recommendation that consensual sex between adult men in private be legalised. However the other side of its effect is to reinstate the integrity of those boundaries – private/public, hidden/exposed, homosexual/heterosexual – which homosexuality was broaching. The criticisms of Rattigan are precisely part of this same desire to divide, clarify and expose.

Many of Rattigan's plays were originally written with explicit homosexual characters (*French Without Tears*, *The Deep Blue Sea* and *Separate Tables*, for example), which he then changed.[38] But many more of them hint at homosexual experiences and activities: the relationship between Tony and David in *First Episode*, the Major in *Follow My Leader* who is blackmailed over an incident in Baghdad ('After all,' he explains, 'a chap's only human, and it was a deuced hot night – '),[39] the suspiciously polymorphous servicemen of *While the Sun Shines*, Alexander the Great and T. E. Lawrence from *Adventure Story* and *Ross*, Mr Miller in *The Deep Blue Sea* and several others. Furthermore, rumours of Rattigan's own bachelor life circulated fairly widely. As indicated above, Rattigan always placed great trust in the audiences of his plays, and it was the audience that had to decode and reinterpret these plays. His plays cannot be judged by the criterion of 'honesty' and 'explicitness' that obsessed a generation after Osborne. They are plays which negotiate sexual desire through structures of hint, implications and metaphor. As David Rudkin has suggested, 'the craftsmanship of which we hear so much loose talk seems to me to arise from deep psychological necessity, a drive to organise the energy that arises out of his own pain. Not to batten it down but to invest it with some expressive clarity that speaks immediately to people, yet keeps itself hidden.'[40]

The shifts in the dominant view of both homosexuality and the theatre that took place in the fifties account for the brutal decline of Rattigan's career. He continued writing, and while *Ross* (1960) was reasonably well received, his ill-judged musical adaptation of *French Without Tears*, *Joie de Vivre* (1960), was a complete disaster, not assisted by a liberal bout of laryngitis among the cast, and the unexpected insanity of the pianist.[41] It ran for four performances.

During the sixties, Rattigan was himself dogged with ill-health: pneumonia and hepatitis were followed by leukaemia. When his death conspicuously failed to transpire, this last diagnosis was admitted to be incorrect. Despite this, he continued to write, producing the successful television play *Heart to Heart* in 1962, and the stage play *Man and Boy* the following year, which received the same sniping that greeted *Variation on a Theme*. In 1964, he wrote *Nelson – a Portrait in Miniature* for Associated Television, as part of a short season of his plays.

It was at this point that Rattigan decided to leave Britain and live abroad. Partly this decision was taken for reasons of health; but partly Rattigan just seemed no longer to be welcome. Ironically, it was the same charge being levelled at Rattigan that he had faced in the thirties, when the newspapers thundered against the those who had supported the Oxford Union's pacifist motion as 'woolly-minded Communists, practical jokers and sexual indeterminates'.[42] As he confessed in an interview late in his life, 'Overnight almost, we were told we were old-fashioned

and effete and corrupt and finished, and... I somehow accepted
Tynan's verdict and went off to Hollywood to write film
scripts.'[43] In 1967 he moved to Bermuda as a tax exile. A stage
adaptation of his Nelson play, as *Bequest to the Nation*, had a
lukewarm reception.

Rattigan had a bad sixties, but his seventies seemed to indicate a
turnaround in his fortunes and reputation. At the end of 1970, a
successful production of *The Winslow Boy* was the first of ten
years of acclaimed revivals. In 1972, Hampstead Theatre revived
While the Sun Shines, and a year later the Young Vic was praised
for its *French Without Tears*. In 1976 and 1977 *The Browning
Version* was revived at the King's Head and *Separate Tables* at
the Apollo. Rattigan briefly returned to Britain in 1971, pulled
partly by his renewed fortune and partly by the fact that he was
given a knighthood in the New Year's honours list. Another
double-bill followed in 1973: *In Praise of Love* comprised the
weak *Before Dawn* and the moving tale of emotional
concealment and creativity, *After Lydia*. Critical reception was
more respectful than usual, although the throwaway farce of the
first play detracted from the quality of the second.

Cause Célèbre, commissioned by BBC Radio and others,
concerned the Rattenbury case, in which Alma Rattenbury's
aged husband was beaten to death by her eighteen-year-old
lover. Shortly after its radio premiere, Rattigan was diagnosed
with bone cancer. Rattigan's response, having been through the
false leukaemia scare in the early sixties, was to greet the news
with unruffled elegance, welcoming the opportunity to 'work
harder and indulge myself more'.[44] The hard work included a
play about the Asquith family and a stage adaptation of *Cause
Célèbre*, but, as production difficulties began to arise over
the latter, the Asquith play slipped out of Rattigan's grasp.
Although very ill, he returned to Britain, and on 4 July 1977, he
was taken by limousine from his hospital bed to Her Majesty's
Theatre, where he watched his last ever premiere. A fortnight
later he had a car drive him around the West End where two of
his plays were then running before boarding the plane for the
last time. On 30 November 1977, in Bermuda, he died.

As Michael Billington's perceptive obituary noted, 'his whole
work is a sustained assault on English middle-class values:

fear of emotional commitment, terror in the face of passion, apprehension about sex'.[45] In death, Rattigan began once again to be seen as someone critically opposed to the values with which he had so long been associated, a writer dramatising dark moments of bleak compassion and aching desire.

Notes

1. Quoted in Rattigan's *Daily Telegraph* obituary (1 December 1977).

2. Michael Darlow and Gillian Hodson. *Terence Rattigan: The Man and His Work*. London and New York: Quartet Books, 1979, p. 26.

3. See, for example, Sheridan Morley. 'Terence Rattigan at 65.' *The Times*. (9 May 1977).

4. Terence Rattigan. Preface. *The Collected Plays of Terence Rattigan: Volume Two*. London: Hamish Hamilton, 1953, p. xv.

5. *Ibid.*, p. viii.

6. *Ibid.*, p. vii.

7. *Ibid.*, p. vii.

8. cf. Sheridan Morley, *op. cit.*

9. Humphrey Carpenter. *OUDS: A Centenary History of the Oxford University Dramatic Society*. With a Prologue by Robert Robinson. Oxford: Oxford University Press, 1985, p. 123.

10. Rattigan may well have reprised this later in life. John Osborne, in his autobiography, recalls a friend showing him a picture of Rattigan performing in an RAF drag show: 'He showed me a photograph of himself with Rattigan, dressed in a *tutu*, carrying a wand, accompanied by a line of aircraftsmen, during which Terry had sung his own show-stopper, 'I'm just about the oldest fairy in the business. I'm quite the oldest fairy that you've ever seen''.' John Osborne. *A Better Class of Person: An Autobiography, Volume I 1929–1956*. London: Faber and Faber, 1981, p. 223.

11. Darlow and Hodson *op. cit.*, p. 83.

12. Norman Gwatkin. Letter to Gilbert Miller, 28 July 1938. in: *Follow My Leader*. Lord Chamberlain's Correspondence: LR 1938. [British Library].

13. Richard Huggett. *Binkie Beaumont: Eminence Grise of the West Theatre 1933–1973*. London: Hodder & Stoughton, 1989, p. 308.

14. Terence Rattigan. Preface. *The Collected Plays of Terence Rattigan: Volume One*. London: Hamish Hamilton, 1953, p. xiv.

15. George Bernard Shaw, in: Keith Newman. *Two Hundred and Fifty Times I Saw a Play: or, Authors, Actors and Audiences*. With the facsimile of a comment by Bernard Shaw. Oxford: Pelagos Press, 1944, p. 2.

16. Henry Channon. *Chips: The Diaries of Sir Henry Channon*. Edited by Robert Rhodes James. Harmondsworth: Penguin, 1974, p. 480. Entry for 29 September 1944.

17. Tom Driberg. *Ruling Passions*. London: Jonathan Cape, 1977, p. 186.

18. See, for example, Norman Hart. 'Introducing Terence Rattigan,' *Theatre World*. xxxi, 171. (April 1939). p. 180 or Ruth Jordan. 'Another Adventure Story,' *Woman's Journal*. (August 1949), pp. 31–32.

19. Audrey Williamson. *Theatre of Two Decades*. New York and London: Macmillan, 1951, p. 100.

20. Terence Rattigan. 'Concerning the Play of Ideas,' *New Statesman and Nation*. (4 March 1950), pp. 241–242.

21 Terence Rattigan. 'The Play of Ideas,' *New Statesman and Nation*. (13 May 1950), pp. 545–546. See also Susan Rusinko, 'Rattigan versus Shaw: The 'Drama of Ideas' Debate'. in: *Shaw: The Annual of Bernard Shaw Studies: Volume Two*. Edited by Stanley Weintraub. University Park, Penn: Pennsylvania State University Press, 1982. pp. 171–78.

22. John Elsom writes that Rattigan's plays 'represented establishment writing'. *Post-War British Drama*. Revised Edition. London: Routledge, 1979, p. 33.

23. B. A. Young. *The Rattigan Version: Sir Terence Rattigan and the Theatre of Character*. Hamish Hamilton: London, 1986, pp. 102–103; and Darlow and Hodson, *op. cit.*, p. 196, 204n.

24. Terence Rattigan. *Coll. Plays: Vol. Two. op. cit.*, pp. xi–xii.

25. *Ibid.,* p. xii.

26. *Ibid.,* p. xiv.

27. *Ibid.,* p. xvi.

28. *Ibid.,* p. xviii.

29. Opened on 17 September 1960. cf. *Plays and Players.* vii, 11 (November 1960).

30. Quoted in Irving Wardle. *The Theatres of George Devine.* London: Jonathan Cape, 1978, p. 180.

31. John Osborne. *Almost a Gentleman: An Autobiography, Volume II 1955–1966.* London: Faber and Faber, 1991, p. 20.

32. Robert Muller. 'Soul-Searching with Terence Rattigan.' *Daily Mail.* (30 April 1960).

33. The headline of Hobson's review in the *Sunday Times,* 11 May 1958.

34. See, for example, Nicholas de Jongh. *Not in Front of the Audience: Homosexuality on Stage.* London: Routledge, 1992, pp. 55–58.

35. Kathleen Tynan. *The Life of Kenneth Tynan.* Corrected Edition. London: Methuen, 1988, p. 118.

36. Cf. Jeffrey Weeks. *Coming Out: Homosexual Politics in Britain from the Nineteenth Century to the Present.* Revised and Updated Edition. London and New York: Quartet, 1990, p. 58; Peter Wildeblood. *Against the Law.* London: Weidenfeld and Nicolson, 1955, p. 46. The story of Gielgud's arrest may be found in Huggett, *op. cit.,* pp. 429–431. It was Gielgud's arrest which apparently inspired Rattigan to write the second part of *Separate Tables,* although again, thanks this time to the Lord Chamberlain, Rattigan had to change the Major's offence to a heterosexual one. See Darlow and Hodson, *op. cit.*, p. 228.

37. See, for example, Rodney Garland's novel about homosexual life in London, *The Heart in Exile.* London: W. H. Allen, 1953, p. 104.

38. See note 36; and also 'Rattigan Talks to John Simon,' *Theatre Arts.* 46 (April 1962), p. 24.

39. Terence Rattigan and Anthony Maurice. *Follow My Leader.* Typescript. Lord Chamberlain Play Collection: 1940/2. Box 2506. [British Library].

40. Quoted in Darlow and Hodson, *op. cit.,* p. 15.

41. B. A. Young, *op. cit.,* p. 162.

42. Quoted in Darlow and Hodson, *op. cit.,* p. 56.

43. Quoted in Sheridan Morley, *op. cit.*

44. Darlow and Hodson, *op. cit.,* p. 308.

45. *Guardian.* (2 December 1977).

List of Rattigan's Produced Plays

TITLE	BRITISH PREMIERE	NEW YORK PREMIERE
First Episode (with Philip Heimann)	Q Theatre, Kew, 11 Sept 1933 (transferred to Comedy Theatre, 26 Jan 1934	Ritz Theatre, 17 Sept 1934
French Without Tears	Criterion Theatre, 6 Nov 1936	Henry Miller Theatre, 28 Sept 1937
After the Dance	St James's Theatre, 21 June 1939	
Follow My Leader (with Anthony Maurice, alias Tony Goldschmidt)	Apollo Theatre, 16 Jan 1940	
Grey Farm (with Hector Bolitho)		Hudson Theatre, 3 May 1940
Flare Path	Apollo Theatre, 13 Aug 1932	Henry Miller Theatre, 23 Dec 1942
While the Sun Shines	Globe Theatre, 24 Dec 1943	Lyceum Theatre, 19 Sept 1944
Love in Idleness	Lyric Theatre, 20 Dec 1944	Empire Theatre (as *O Mistress Mine*), 23 Jan 1946
The Winslow Boy	Lyric Theatre, 23 May 1946	Empire Theatre, 29 Oct 1947
Playbill (*The Browning Version* and *Harlequinade*)	Phoenix Theatre, 8 Sept 1948	Coronet Theatre, 12 Oct 1949
Adventure Story	St James's Theatre, 17 March 1949	
A Tale of Two Cities (from Charles Dickens, with John Gielgud)	St Brendan's College Dramatic Society, Clifton, 23 Jan 1950	
Who is Sylvia?	Criterion Theatre, 24 Oct 1950	

Final Test (TV)	BBC TV, 29 July 1951	
The Deep Blue Sea	Duchess Theatre, 6 Mar 1952	Morosco Theatre, 5 Nov 1952
The Sleeping Prince	Phoenix Theatre, 5 Nov 1953	Coronet Theatre, 1 Nov 1956
Seperate Tables (*The Table by the Window* and *Table Number Seven*)	St James's Theatre, 22 Sept 1954	Music Box Theatre, 25 Oct 1956
Variation on a Theme	Globe Theatre, 8 May 1958	
Ross	Theatre Royal Haymarket 12 May 1960	Eugene O'Neill Theatre 26 Dec 1961
Joie de Vivre (with Robert Stolz and Paul Dehn)	Queen's Theatre, 14 July 1960	
Heart to Heart (TV)	BBC TV, 6 Dec 1962	
Man and Boy	Queen's Theatre, 4 Sept 1963	Brooks Atkinson Theatre, 12 Nov 1963
Ninety Years On (TV)	BBC TV, 29 Nov 1964	
Nelson – A Portrait in Miniature (TV)	Associated Television, 21 Mar 1966	
All On Her Own (TV) (adapted for the stage as *Duologue*)	BBC 2, 25 Sept 1968	
A Bequest to the Nation	Theatre Royal Haymarket 23 Sept 1970	
High Summer (TV)	Thames TV, 12 Sept 1972	
In Praise of Love (*After Lydia* and *Before Dawn*)	Duchess Theatre, 27 Sept 1973	Morosco Theatre, 10 Dec 1974
Cause Célèbre (radio)	BBC Radio 4, 27 Oct 1975	
Duologue	King's Head Theatre, 21 Feb 1976	
Cause Célèbre (stage)	Her Majesty's Theatre, 4 July 1977	
Less Than Kind	Jermyn Street Theatre, 20 January 2011	

THE DEEP BLUE SEA

Terence Rattigan

To Mr and Mrs Newport
My host and hostess at The Stag and Hounds, Binfield.
With affection and gratitude.

Characters

MRS ELTON
PHILIP WELCH
ANN WELCH
HESTER COLLYER
MR MILLER
WILLIAM COLLYER
FREDDIE PAGE
JACKIE JACKSON

Act One   *Morning*
Act Two   *Afternoon*
Act Three   *Evening*

*The action passes during the course of a day in September in
the sitting-room of a furnished flat in the north-west of London.*

The Deep Blue Sea was first produced at the Duchess Theatre,
London, on 6 March 1952, with the following cast:

PHILIP WELCH	David Aylmer
MRS ELTON	Barbara Leake
ANN WELCH	Ann Walford
HESTER COLLYER	Peggy Ashcroft
MR MILLER	Peter Illing
WILLIAM COLLYER	Roland Culver
FREDDIE PAGE	Kenneth More
JACKIE JACKSON	Raymond Francis

The play directed by Frith Banbury
Setting by Tanya Moiseiwitsch

ACT ONE

Scene: the sitting-room of a furnished flat in the north-west of London. It is a big room for it is on the first floor of a large and gloomy Victorian mansion, converted to flats after World War I, but it has an air of dinginess, even of squalor, heightened by the fact that it has, like its immediate badly-blitzed neighbourhood, so obviously 'come down in the world'.

There is a door backstage right, leading on to the first-floor landing of the house, and another backstage left, leading into the bedroom. Between them is another small door, evidently put in when the house was converted and which gives access to a tiny kitchen.

There is a window right, curtained at the moment, and in the left wall is a fireplace, originally designed for coal, but now occupied by a gas-fire. On the floor in front of this, dimly seen in the darkened room, lies HESTER COLLYER, *with her head, covered by a rug, very close to the unlit stove.*

There is the sound of voices on the landing outside. A young man (PHILIP) *can be heard calling and a woman* (MRS ELTON) *answering.*

PHILIP (*off*). Mrs Elton! Mrs Elton!

MRS ELTON (*off*). Yes, Mr Welch?

PHILIP (*off*). I think it's coming from here.

MRS ELTON (*off*). From Number Three? I'll just come up.

There is a pause, and then another voice (ANN*'s*) *can be heard from farther away.*

ANN (*off*). What's the matter?

PHILIP (*off*). Escape of gas, darling. Don't light a match or anything, will you?

ANN (*off*). Well, it's not us, I know that.

PHILIP (*off*). No, it's in here –

There is a series of knocks on the door.

MRS ELTON (*off – calling*). Isn't there any answer? Mr Page?
. . . Mrs Page? (*There is no reply. Off.*) It's all right. I've got
the pass key.

*There is the sound of a key in the lock, and the door opens,
revealing* MRS ELTON *on the threshold. She is caretaker-
housekeeper to the flats, and is in the middle fifties. Behind
her is* PHILIP WELCH, *aged about twenty-four and, from
his clothes, an office worker.*

Phew! It's here all right. They must have left something on.
Wicked waste – (*She comes into the room.*)

PHILIP. Careful, Mrs Elton. Put something over your mouth –

MRS ELTON. Oh, it's not as bad as that. Coming from the
kitchen I expect –

*She reaches the window, draws the curtains briskly, and
flings up the window.*

Left his cooker on all night, I shouldn't be surprised. Comes
in late, a bit the worse for you know what, and makes himself a cup of tea – and turns on all the taps in sight.
Someone'll blow this whole house up one of these days –
that's what'll happen –

*While muttering she has been going towards the kitchen
door. She opens it and goes inside. Meanwhile* PHILIP *has
taken a step or two inside the room, and now sees the
prostrate* HESTER *by the fire.*

PHILIP. My God! (*He runs up to her; calling urgently.*) Mrs
Elton!

MRS ELTON *emerges from the kitchen.*

MRS ELTON. It's not in here –

PHILIP. Mrs Elton! Quick. Get a doctor or someone –

He raises HESTER*'s head away from the fire, and pulls the
rug off her.*

MRS ELTON. Oh heavens!

PHILIP (*fumbling for the gas faucet*). Where does this thing turn off?

MRS ELTON. Mrs Page! Mrs Page! (She *takes* HESTER*'s hand.*) She's not dead, is she?

PHILIP. I don't know. I don't think so. (*In a panic.*) This isn't turned off. I can't turn it off.

MRS ELTON. Here. Let me. It *is* off. (*She turns the faucet both ways.*) It wasn't on.

PHILIP. It must have been.

MRS ELTON. It's the meter then. It must have switched itself off at the meter.

PHILIP. Help me get her to the window. You take her feet.

MRS ELTON. Oh the poor thing! Why did she have to go and do it? What's the point in doing a thing like this?

PHILIP *is supporting her shoulders. We see now that she is dressed in a crumpled day dress.* MRS ELTON *takes her feet and between them they carry her towards the window.*

PHILIP. Let's get her into this chair. Better turn it round to face the window. All right. I've got her.

MRS ELTON. This'll mean the police. In twenty-three years Mr Elton and me have never had a speck of trouble in these flats, and now – Mrs Page – of all people –

PHILIP *and* MRS ELTON *lower* HESTER *into the chair.* ANN, PHILIP*'s young wife, also an office worker, appears on the landing outside.*

ANN (*calling*). Philip? Are you in there?

PHILIP. Yes. Don't come in.

ANN. We'll be late for the office –

PHILIP. You go on. Tell them I'll get there as soon as I can.

ANN. Is anything wrong? (*She comes into the room.*)

PHILIP (*savagely*). I said not to come in.

ANN *sees* HESTER *and runs over to her.*

ANN. Gas?

PHILIP (*slightly surprised at his wife's composure*). Yes.

MRS ELTON. She's breathing.

PHILIP. Where's the nearest doctor?

MRS ELTON. Dr. Brown. No – he's on his holiday. I know.
Mr Miller. I'll get him.

ANN. Mr Miller upstairs, you mean?

MRS ELTON (*on her way to the door*). Yes.

ANN. But he's not a doctor.

MRS ELTON *has run out, and we can hear her calling:* 'Mr
Miller! Mr Miller!' *as she goes upstairs.*

She's hysterical, Philip. Mr Miller's not a doctor –

PHILIP *has gone back to the gas-fire, while* ANN *stays at
the armchair.*

PHILIP. See this? (*He picks up a little empty bottle from the
floor.*) Aspirin. Empty.

ANN. Oh Lord!

PHILIP. And here's the glass. (*He picks up a glass.*) She ground
them in here. Look.

ANN. She must have wanted to dope herself, before the gas –

PHILIP. The gas was off. The tap was turned on, but the gas was
off. It must have run out in the meter –

ANN. Where's her husband?

PHILIP. I don't know. (*He opens the bedroom door and looks
inside.*) The bed hasn't been slept in.

ANN. We ought to get hold of him somehow.

PHILIP. Yes, but how?

ANN (*excitedly*). She's opened her eyes.

PHILIP *joins* ANN *at the chair.*

Mrs Page! Mrs Page!

HESTER (*speaking in a low, thick murmur, the words barely distinguishable.*) Finished – Freddie – finished –

PHILIP. Mrs Page – it's all right – everything's all right, now –

HESTER (*with a low moan*). If you – only would – understand – how happy – like sleep – Freddie – sleep – you must understand – forgive bad writing – poor Freddie – poor darling Freddie –

She moans again, as if in a bad dream, and closes her eyes, shaking her head.

ANN. Don't worry, Mrs Page. You mustn't worry. You're among friends –

MR MILLER, unshaven and in a shabby dressing-gown, comes in hurriedly followed by MRS ELTON. He is about forty and when he speaks it is possible to detect a slight German accent. He is carrying a battered instrument case. He goes over to the chair and pushes ANN and PHILIP rather brusquely out of the way, before kneeling down in front of HESTER. With quick deft movements he makes an obviously practised and professional, if cursory, examination.

ANN. She came to, a moment ago, and talked. She kept on saying Freddie. And something about being happy – like sleep –

PHILIP. And then she said something about bad writing.

ANN. Forgive her bad writing, it was.

PHILIP. I didn't hear forgive. I just heard – bad writing. We found this on the floor.

He hands him the aspirin bottle. MILLER nods and slips it into his pocket. Then suddenly he slaps HESTER's face hard. She opens her eyes, bewildered. MILLER takes the aspirin bottle from his pocket and holds it up before her eyes.

MILLER. How many?

HESTER closes her eyes. MILLER slaps her again.

How many?

HESTER (*quite clearly*). Twelve. (*She closes her eyes again.*)

MILLER (*to* MRS ELTON). Where's the bedroom?

MRS ELTON (*hustling to open the door*). In here.

> MILLER *slips his arms underneath* HESTER'*s body and carries her to the door.*

MILLER (*to* MRS ELTON). Bring my case, would you please.

> *He goes, with his burden, towards the bedroom.* PHILIP
> *picks up his case.*

(*As he goes.*) A glass of hot water, please, Mrs Elton.

> *He goes into the bedroom, followed by* PHILIP.

MRS ELTON. Yes, straight away.

> *She comes back into the sitting-room, and goes into the
> kitchen.* PHILIP *emerges from the bedroom.*

PHILIP. Look, darling, hadn't you better get on to the office?
It's all right for me, but I don't like the idea of you being
late.

ANN. They'll understand. There's never much in on Mondays,
and after all a suicide doesn't happen every day.

PHILIP (*with a glance at the bedroom door*). He seems to know
his job all right. Let's hope it's just attempted suicide.

ANN. Poor soul. I wonder what made her do it. Freddie – that's
her husband, I suppose?

PHILIP. I think so, yes. I've seen his letters downstairs.
Frederick Page, Esq.

ANN. I've never liked the look of him.

PHILIP. She said 'poor darling Freddie'. That doesn't sound as
if he'd deserted her, or anything.

ANN. Then where is he?

PHILIP. Husbands do, you know, occasionally go off on
business without taking their wives.

MRS ELTON *comes out of the kitchen with a glass of warm water. She crosses to the bedroom door, knocks, and goes in.*

ANN. I wish we could help, somehow.

She is looking at the fireplace and notices something. She goes quickly over and takes a letter off the mantelpiece.

ANN. Yes. Of course.

PHILIP. What?

ANN (*holding up the letter*). Suicide note. We should have thought of that.

PHILIP. Who's it addressed to?

ANN (*reading*). 'Freddie'. It's in pencil – very faint.

PHILIP. 'Forgive my bad writing'. I expect that's in it. She'd probably taken the aspirin.

ANN. Should we open it?

PHILIP. No. It may be wanted by the police.

ANN. The police? Oh dear.

PHILIP (*unhappily*). I suppose we ought to ring them up.

She puts it back quickly on the mantelpiece.

ANN. It's a sordid business, isn't it, a suicide? I wonder if they think of that when they do it – police and coroners and things. I suppose we'll have to give evidence.

PHILIP. If there's an inquest, yes. But let's pray it doesn't come to that.

ANN. Attempted suicide is a crime, anyway, isn't it? People get jailed for it, don't they?

PHILIP. Yes.

ANN. Well, then, you mustn't ring up the police. Not yet anyway.

PHILIP. We ought to get in touch with somebody, though. I wish to God her husband would come. That letter proves he

hadn't deserted her. She expected him. Put it back exactly
where you found it, darling.

ANN. I did.

PHILIP. No. Only a bit of it was showing. It was half behind
that clock –

ANN *gingerly puts the letter in the indicated position.* MRS
ELTON *comes out of the bedroom.*

(*To* MRS ELTON.) How is she?

MRS ELTON. He didn't say, but she's looking better. He's
given her an injection of something. That made her sick. I've
got to make some black coffee.

She goes back into the kitchen, PHILIP *follows her to the
door.*

(*Off.*) There's some here ready. I'll just need to warm it up –

PHILIP (*calling after her*). Mrs Elton, we both think we ought
to get hold of Mr Page. Have you any idea where he might
be?

MRS ELTON *appears at the door.*

MRS ELTON. No. I can't say I have.

PHILIP. Does he go away often?

MRS ELTON. Now and then. Not for more than a night usually
–

PHILIP. Where does he work?

MRS ELTON. I don't know that he does work – not regularly
that is. He's often here all day, I know that. I believe he's
something to do with aeroplanes – or used to be, anyway.

PHILIP. Selling them?

MRS ELTON. No. Flying them, I think. Test pilot – isn't that
what they call it?

PHILIP. Yes. You don't know for which company?

MRS ELTON. No. Besides, I tell you, I don't think he's doing it
any more –

She goes back into the kitchen.

ANN. She must have some relations in London we could get hold of.

PHILIP. Yes. (*He goes to the kitchen door again. Calling.*) Mrs Elton. Do you know if Mrs Page has any relations in London?

MRS ELTON *reappears and comes in, leaving the kitchen door open.*

MRS ELTON. No. I can't say I do.

PHILIP. Can you think of any particular friend then? Haven't you ever heard her talk about anybody?

MRS ELTON. No. Always kept herself very much to herself, Mrs Page.

ANN. She must have had visitors –

MRS ELTON. Hardly at all, and they always asked for him – not for her.

PHILIP. What were their names?

MRS ELTON. I can't remember.

PHILIP. Do try and help, Mrs Elton. This is desperately important.

MRS ELTON. I'm sorry, Mr Welch. It's the shock.

PHILIP. Yes, yes of course. But now look. Think hard. Don't you know of anyone connected with Mrs Page we might get into touch with?

ANN. Solicitor – bank manager –

Pause. MRS ELTON *frowns in concentration.*

MRS ELTON (*at length.*) There *is* her husband, of course –

PHILIP (*with a hopeless gesture*). I know – but we haven't an idea where he is –

MRS ELTON. I didn't mean – (*She looks alarmed.*) No, I can't think of anyone. (*She turns to go back into the kitchen.*)

ANN (*sharply*). Mrs Elton. What did you mean by 'There *is* her husband'?

MRS ELTON *turns slowly.*

Isn't Mr Page her husband?

Pause.

PHILIP. What's her real name?

MRS ELTON. I haven't said anything.

PHILIP. Look, Mrs Elton. If the police come, it'll all have to come out anyway. You don't need to tell us anything you don't want to; but I do think that if you know her real husband you ought to ring him up and tell him what's happened.

MRS ELTON. I don't know her real husband. And what I do know I promised faithfully I'd never tell a living soul. It was all because I picked up her ration book one day, and then she told me straight out quite simply all about it – how she hadn't been able to get herself a divorce. Poor lamb – she thought Mr Elton would turn her out. I found her that evening packing her things. I told her not to be silly. As if I'd tell Mr Elton a thing like that. It's none of his business, or mine, or anyone else's, come to that.

She goes into the kitchen. PHILIP *and* ANN *exchange a glance.*

ANN. I'm sure I'm right now, Philip. This man Page has deserted her, and she had no one to turn to. She's probably quarrelled with her family, and her friends have dropped her, most likely –

MRS ELTON *emerges with a cup and saucer on a tray.*

MRS ELTON. So you think I ought to tell her husband about this?

PHILIP. Well, yes, Mrs Elton. It seems to me the only thing to do.

MRS ELTON. All right. You do it. I wouldn't know how. Her name is Collyer – *(Spelling it.)* C-O-L-L-Y-E-R, and her husband's name's in the papers quite often. She showed me once. They call him Mr Justice Collyer – so I suppose he's a judge.

ANN. Sir William Collyer.

MRS ELTON. That's right. Sir William Collyer.

She goes into the bedroom.

PHILIP (*awed*). Gosh!

ANN. Do you think you dare, Philip?

PHILIP. I don't see why not.

He has grasped a telephone book and is looking through it.

ANN (*in a panic*). Whatever you do, don't tell him you work at the Home Office.

PHILIP (*he looks at his watch*). Quarter past nine. We ought to get him at his home. Here we are – Collyer – William – there are two, but one's in Chiswick. Eaton Square – that's the one. (*He dials a number.*)

ANN *waits by his side.*

(*At length.*) Hullo. Could I speak to Sir William Collyer, please? . . . No, I'd rather not give my name. Just tell him that it's very urgent indeed, and that it concerns his wife . . . His wife . . . Yes. I'll wait.

He takes ANN'*s hand and presses it affectionately. He is evidently rather enjoying his strong male act and knows that he is impressing* ANN.

Hullo! Sir William Collyer? I'm afraid I have some serious news for you. Your wife has been concerned in – an accident . . . It's rather difficult to tell you that on the telephone . . . Well, if you insist. Gas poisoning, and an overdose of drugs . . . No, but very ill . . . No. She doesn't know I'm telephoning . . . He's not here . . . 27 Weybridge Villas, Ladbroke Grove . . . Yes. Flat Number Three, first floor . . . You'll find the front-door open. Yes. There's a doctor – that's to say, she's being given medical attention now. (*He rings off.*) He's coming round at once.

ANN. Did he seem upset?

PHILIP. It was rather difficult to tell. He asked if Page was here.

MRS ELTON *comes out of the bedroom.*

I've rung him up, Mrs Elton. He's coming round.

MRS ELTON (*slowly*). I only hope we've done the right thing.

ANN. I think we have.

PHILIP. How is she?

MRS ELTON. Sitting up now. Drank her coffee quite peace-
fully. Of course – still very weak.

ANN. Don't you think we ought to get her a proper doctor?

MRS ELTON. I've got far more faith in Mr Miller than in any
proper doctor thank you very much. He's done a sight more
for Mr Elton than any of those Harley Street specialists ever
did – five guineas or no five guineas.

PHILIP. How is Mr Elton?

MRS ELTON. Well, he'd be much better if it weren't for this
damp weather. Shocking for arthritis, it's been. I've been
fixing his pillows all night long. (*She goes to the door.*)
Well, I've got to give Number Six his tea and I haven't
started on my hall yet. Give me a shout if I'm wanted, will
you.

PHILIP *and* ANN *nod.* MILLER *comes out of the bedroom.*

Will you be wanting me for anything more?

MILLER. No, Mrs Elton.

MRS ELTON. I'll leave this door on the latch.

She goes out.

MILLER (*to* PHILIP). Have you a cigarette?

PHILIP. Yes, indeed. (*He brings out a small packet.* MILLER
takes a cigarette and lights it.) My name is Welch. I live
upstairs in Number Five. This is my wife.

MILLER *nods to* ANN.

MILLER. Are you friends of hers?

ANN. No. My husband found Mrs Page this morning and we
were just waiting around to see if there's anything we can do.

MILLER. There is nothing you can do.

ANN (*appalled*). You don't mean she's dying?

MILLER (*smiling*). On the contrary.

PHILIP. She'll recover?

MILLER. Sixty grains of aspirin are hardly enough to kill a healthy child, and the symptoms of gas poisoning are very slight –

PHILIP. That's because the gas gave out at the meter.

MILLER. Yes. She couldn't have bungled it worse, could she? I must go back to my breakfast and I'm sure there is no reason whatever for your staying here any longer. Good morning.

ANN. But is she really all right?

MILLER. I've told you. After twenty-four hours in bed she will be completely recovered.

ANN. Yes – her body. But what about her mind?

MILLER (*Amused*). You make that distinction? Her mind is perfectly sound. There is no trace whatever of any psychotic symptoms which might justify a certificate of insanity.

ANN. Yes – but she did try to kill herself, didn't she?

MILLER. It would seem so.

ANN. Well – what made her do that?

MILLER (*after a slight pause*). She wanted to die, I suppose.

PHILIP. But mightn't she try to do it again, Doctor?

MILLER. I'm not a doctor.

PHILIP. No. Don't you think she might try to do it again?

MILLER. I'm not a prophet either. In fact I make a fairly respectable living out of other people's pretensions to prophecy. Still, if you want me to be a punter for once, I would say that she probably will try again, and try again very soon.

ANN (*indignantly*). But isn't there anything we can do about it?

MILLER. (*gently shaking his head*). No.

He goes out.

PHILIP. Well, there's a callous swine, if you like.

ANN. He's phoney, that man. I'm certain he is. He was just trying to impress us with all that stuff about psychoses and things. Of course she's ill. Of course she needs looking after.

The bedroom door opens and HESTER *comes out. She is in a dressing-gown, but has tidied her hair, and put on make-up. Now that we see her under more normal circumstances we find that she is in the middle thirties with a thoughtful, remote face that has no pretensions to great beauty.*

Oh! Should you be out of bed?

HESTER. I came for a cigarette. There was a packet here last night, I think.

PHILIP. Have one of these. (*He extends his packet.*)

HESTER. No, I won't smoke yours. I know I brought a packet in with me. (*She searches on the table.*) Ah yes. Here they are.

She takes a cigarette. PHILIP *lights it for her.*

Thank you so much. You're Mr Welch, aren't you? We met downstairs once, do you remember?

PHILIP. Yes, that's right.

HESTER. And is this Mrs Welch?

ANN. Yes.

HESTER. How do you do? Do you mind if I sit down? I'm still feeling a little strange. (*She sits down.*)

ANN. Don't you think you ought to go back to bed?

HESTER. Oh no. I feel much better sitting up, thank you.

PHILIP. You've been very ill, you know.

HESTER. Oh no. Just a bit dopey, that's all. Idiotic accident, wasn't it? I'm terribly sorry for all the trouble I've caused –

PHILIP *and* ANN (*murmuring*). That's quite all right.

HESTER. I don't know how it could possibly have happened. I'd been out to a cinema, by myself, and I came back here. I remember thinking it was a bit chilly and I turned on the gas-fire to light it, and after that, as they say in novels, I knew no more. I couldn't find the matches, I suppose, and the fumes must have put me out –

ANN (*rather crossly*). It was lucky for you that you didn't put a shilling in the meter first.

HESTER. The meter?

PHILIP. Yes. The gas cut off automatically.

HESTER. Oh. That's what happened, is it? (*After a pause.*) Yes. That was lucky. (*She leans back in the chair and closes her eyes.*)

ANN. Are you sure you're feeling all right?

HESTER (*opening her eyes*). Perfectly all right, thank you.

ANN. Don't you think you ought to see a proper doctor?

HESTER. Haven't I just seen a proper doctor?

ANN. He's only an amateur. Bookmaker's clerk or something.

HESTER. A strange hobby for a bookmaker's clerk. He seemed very efficient. Horribly efficient. Look, I'm sure I'm keeping you both, and there's really no need to stay. It's been very kind of you.

PHILIP. Well – (*He looks to* ANN *for support.*) The fact is I have something to tell you.

HESTER*'s eyes are wandering over the room.* ANN *is watching her.*

ANN. Are you looking for something?

HESTER. Yes. I think I left a letter lying around somewhere.

ANN *goes to the mantelpiece and takes the letter from behind the clock.*

ANN. Is this it? (*She hands it to her.*)

HESTER (*gazing at it casually*). Yes. That's the one.

She slips it into her dressing-gown pocket.

(*Politely to* PHILIP.) You were going to tell me something?

PHILIP. You may be very angry with me.

HESTER. I hope not.

PHILIP. I hope not, too. When we found you this morning you
seemed – very ill – almost at death's door, in fact –

HESTER *glances at the fireplace, but says nothing.* PHILIP
continues after a pause.

Mr Page was away, and we didn't know where to get hold of
him –

HESTER. You should have asked me. He's at the King's Head
Hotel, at Sunningdale.

ANN (*quickly*). Are you expecting him back this morning?

HESTER. No, I think he's playing golf. (*Smiling.*) I'm a golf
widow, you know, Mrs Welch. Every weekend I'm deserted.
It's shocking. (*To* PHILIP.) Go on.

PHILIP (*desperately*). Well, I felt it my duty to get in touch with
someone. We didn't know where your parents lived –

HESTER. They're both dead anyway.

PHILIP. Or any of your friends.

HESTER *nods.*

So I'm afraid I took it on myself to ring up – Sir William
Collyer.

There is a pause. HESTER *gets up and puts out her
cigarette.*

HESTER. What did you tell him?

PHILIP. That there'd been an accident.

HESTER. Did you give him this address?

PHILIP. Yes. He's coming round.

HESTER. How soon?

PHILIP. He said, at once.

> HESTER *looks at the bedroom door, as if meditating whether she has time for flight.*

> I'm sorry if I've done wrong. I couldn't know, you see.

HESTER. No, you couldn't.

ANN (*loyally*). It was mainly my responsibility, Lady Collyer. It was I who told Philip he ought to ring up.

HESTER. Yes, I see. Do you mind not using that name?

ANN. I'm sorry.

HESTER. It was Mrs Elton who told you?

PHILIP. She slipped it out by accident. I may say your secret is absolutely safe with both Ann and myself.

HESTER (*with a faint smile*). My guilty secret? That's very kind of you both.

PHILIP (*stiffly*). Well, I think we must be going. Come along, Ann.

> ANN *and* PHILIP *go to the door.*

HESTER (*with contrition*). Goodbye. You've been very kind, and I'm grateful.

PHILIP. There's no need. Let me know if there's anything I can do, won't you?

HESTER. There is something you can do. Don't breathe a word of this stupid – accident – to anyone – to anyone else, that is.

PHILIP. I won't.

HESTER. Do you know my – do you know Freddie Page?

PHILIP. No.

HESTER. If ever you should meet him you will, above all, be particularly careful not to mention anything of this to him, won't you? It might – it might alarm him – quite unnecessarily.

ANN. We won't say a word – either of us.

HESTER. Thank you. Goodbye.

PHILIP. Goodbye.

ANN. Goodbye – Mrs Page.

She follows PHILIP *out.* HESTER, *after a moment, goes out on to the landing.*

HESTER (*calling*). Mrs Elton! Mrs Elton!

MRS ELTON (*off*). Coming, dear. (*She comes in.*) You're up. I'm sure you shouldn't be.

HESTER (*abruptly*). Mrs Elton, if Sir William Collyer comes, I don't want to see him.

MRS ELTON. I'm sorry about that. They got it out of me –

HESTER. Yes, I know.

MRS ELTON. What shall I tell him?

HESTER. Anything you like – provided I don't have to see him.

MRS ELTON. Yes, dear. I understand. Would you like me to make you some more coffee?

HESTER. No, thank you, Mrs Elton. There's nothing I want at all.

MRS ELTON. When's Mr Page coming home?

HESTER. I don't know. Some time this evening, I expect.

MRS ELTON. I'll come and sit with you, if you like, until then. I've just got to finish my work –

HESTER. It's very kind of you, Mrs Elton, but I shall be perfectly all right alone.

MRS ELTON (*doubtfully*). Will you, dear? Are you sure?

HESTER. Yes. You can trust me.

MRS ELTON. Oh, I didn't mean that –

HESTER (*gently*). Didn't you?

MRS ELTON (*angrily*). Whatever possessed you to do a dreadful thing like that?

Pause.

HESTER (*lying back with her eyes closed*). The devil I suppose.

MRS ELTON. I should just think it was. Are you a Catholic?

HESTER (*sleepily*). No. I didn't mean that kind of devil. Or is it the same kind? Anyway when you're between any kind of devil and the deep blue sea, the deep blue sea sometimes looks very inviting. It did last night.

MRS ELTON. I can't make you out. You're not a wicked woman – and yet what you did last night was wicked – wicked and cruel. Now supposing it had been Mr Page and not you that we'd found lying there this morning, how would *you* have felt?

HESTER. Very, very surprised.

MRS ELTON. Nothing more?

HESTER. Oh yes. A lot more. A whole universe more. (*With a faint smile.*) He's not lying there. He's playing golf.

Pause. MRS ELTON *is looking at her, puzzled.*

And when he comes back from golf, he must know nothing of what happened last night. Do you understand, Mrs Elton? Nothing.

MRS ELTON. If that's the way you want it.

HESTER. That's the way I want it.

Pause.

MRS ELTON. It's not money, is it, dear?

HESTER. No. It's not money.

MRS ELTON. Because if it is, I was going to say – about this flat –

HESTER (*quickly interrupting*). It's very kind of you, Mrs
Elton, and I'm deeply grateful. But I couldn't accept it.
I know we owe you a month's rent – but it will be paid,
I promise you, in a day or two – As a matter of fact I've got
someone who's very interested in those two pictures there.
(*She points to two pictures on the wall.*)

MRS ELTON. Oh yes. Very nice. (*Pointing to one.*) That's a
pier, isn't it?

HESTER. Weymouth Pier.

MRS ELTON (*politely*). Oh yes. You can tell at once. Very
clever. How much would you get for a thing like that?

HESTER. Well – for the two I'm asking twenty-five pounds.

MRS ELTON. Are you, really? Well, I never. (*After a slight
pause.*) Excuse me asking you, won't you – but is Mr Page in
a job just now?

HESTER. Not exactly. Not at the moment. But – he has
interests in the city – you know.

MRS ELTON (*who has evidently heard this one before*). Oh
yes? Well, perhaps he'll get himself something steady soon.
It shouldn't be too hard these days –

*She moves towards the door, then stops at the sound of a
loud knock on the door. MRS ELTON waves HESTER out of
sight of the door and goes to open it. COLLYER –
a forceful-looking figure in the middle forties, dressed in
short morning coat and striped trousers – stands on the
threshold.*

COLLYER. Mrs Page?

MRS ELTON. I'm sorry, sir – you can't come in. Mrs Page is
too ill to be bothered –

*COLLYER brushes her impatiently aside and walks into the
room. He sees HESTER at once. They stare at each other
without speaking. MRS ELTON flutters helplessly between
them.*

COLLYER (*to* HESTER). Tell her to go.

HESTER. It's all right, Mrs Elton. Thank you.

MRS ELTON *shrugs her shoulders and departs.* COLLYER *and* HESTER *still stare at each other. HESTER's alarm, now that she is finally confronted with her husband, seems to have dissipated.*

COLLYER. Are you all right?

HESTER. Quite all right.

COLLYER. What happened?

HESTER. How much did that boy tell you on the telephone?

COLLYER. Enough to spare you the necessity of lying to me.

HESTER. I must be careful what I say. Attempted suicide is a crime, isn't it?

COLLYER. Yes.

HESTER. And I'm speaking to a judge.

COLLYER. You're speaking to your husband.

HESTER. Shall we say, *crise de nerfs?*

COLLYER. Nonsense. You're as sane a person as any in the world.

HESTER. Perhaps I've changed since I left you, Bill. No, I'd better not say that. It might give you an opportunity of saying I told you so.

COLLYER. You misjudge me.

HESTER. Misjudge a judge? Isn't that *lèse-majesté?*

There is a pause while HESTER *stares at him.*

COLLYER. Why didn't you let me know you were in London?

HESTER. The last time I saw you you said you never wanted to hear from me again.

COLLYER. The last time I saw you I didn't know what I was saying. How long have you been back from Canada?

HESTER. Oh, three or four months now. Freddie lost his job you see – that's to say he gave it up – it wasn't a very good one – and we neither of us liked Ottawa very much –

COLLYER. Why didn't you answer my letter?

HESTER. I never got a letter.

COLLYER. Oh, didn't you? I addressed it to the aircraft firm in Ottawa, and put 'please forward'.

HESTER. Oh. We left rather hurriedly, and I forgot to leave a forwarding address. What did you say in the letter, Bill?

COLLYER. Just that you could have your divorce if you still wanted it.

HESTER. Oh!

COLLYER. Not getting a reply I'm afraid I've taken no steps.

HESTER. No. That was generous of you, Bill. Still I should have thought what you said before about the scandal would be even more operative now that you're a judge.

COLLYER. What I said before was exaggerated. I wanted to put every difficulty in your way that I possibly could.

HESTER. Sit down, Bill, now you're here. It's nice to see you again. Have a cigarette?

COLLYER (*ignoring the proffered packet*). No thank you. (*He lights her cigarette.*) Has he deserted you?

HESTER. He's playing golf at Sunningdale. He plays there a lot these days. I wonder you haven't run into him.

COLLYER. I haven't ever been to Sunningdale since –

HESTER. You still feel so strongly?

COLLYER. You know I do.

HESTER. I know you did – but after all this time? I suppose ten months isn't very long. I keep thinking it's so much longer.

COLLYER. Has it seemed so much longer?

HESTER (*quietly*). Yes, Bill. Almost a lifetime.

Pause.

COLLYER. Is he being unfaithful to you?

HESTER. No.

COLLYER. He still loves you?

HESTER (*after a slight pause*). As much as he did ten months ago.

COLLYER. And you still love him?

HESTER. Yes, Bill. I still love him.

COLLYER. Is it money?

HESTER. No. It isn't money.

COLLYER. He's still got a job?

HESTER. Not as a test pilot. He gave that up some time ago. He's – he's working in the city now, you know.

COLLYER. In a job in which they allow him to play golf on Mondays?

HESTER. Well – it's a sort of free-lance job, you see.

COLLYER. Yes. I see. What salary –

HESTER. You're on the wrong track, Bill. All right. We do owe a month's rent, but money had nothing to do with it.

COLLYER. What was it then?

HESTER. Bill, I'm not in the witness box and you'll never get me to confess that I had any reason for trying to kill myself last night. Any logical reason, that is.

COLLYER. But you did try to kill yourself?

HESTER. While the balance of my mind was temporarily disturbed. Isn't that the legal phrase?

COLLYER. What was it that disturbed the balance of your mind?

HESTER. Oh dear, oh dear, I don't know. A great tidal wave of illogical emotions.

COLLYER. Can you give a name to those emotions?

HESTER. Yes, I suppose so. Anger, hatred and shame – in about equal parts I think.

COLLYER. Anger – at Page?

HESTER. Yes.

COLLYER. And hatred – ?

HESTER. Of myself, of course. (*Pause.*) Shame at being alive.

COLLYER. I see.

HESTER. Do you?

COLLYER. No, I suppose I don't. Can I do anything to help?

HESTER. No, Bill. Nobody can.

COLLYER. Well – at least I've found you again.

HESTER. Were you looking so very hard?

COLLYER. No. You see, rather foolishly I thought my indifference would hurt your vanity.

HESTER *only smiles in reply.*

You must understand that I'm very inexperienced in matters of this kind.

HESTER (*gently*). So am I, Bill. Almost as inexperienced as yourself.

She touches his arm sympathetically. He takes hold of a bracelet she is wearing.

COLLYER. I'm glad you still wear it.

HESTER. What? (*Remembering with an effort.*) Oh yes, of course. An anniversary present, wasn't it?

COLLYER. Our seventh.

HESTER (*awkwardly*). It was a good party we gave that night. All our nicest friends, weren't they?

COLLYER *nods.*

I read Sibyl's new book. I didn't think it was as good as her last. Tell me, is David very pompous now he's Solicitor-General?

COLLYER. No. Not very.

HESTER. Is Alice still as gay as ever? (COLLYER *nods.*) Oh dear. (*She sighs nostalgically.*) Didn't I make a speech that night?

COLLYER. Yes. Old Lord Marsden was wildly impressed.

HESTER. That's what comes of being a clergyman's daughter. I could always impress your erudite friends, when put to it. I only wish I were as good with Freddie's friends.

COLLYER. Aren't you?

HESTER. Oh no. On pub crawls I'm a terrible fish out of water.

COLLYER. Pub crawls?

HESTER. Oh, you needn't be shocked. There's nothing in the the world more respectable than pub crawls. More respectable or more unspeakably dreary.

Pause.

COLLYER. Hester –

HESTER. Yes?

COLLYER. It doesn't matter. The question I was going to ask you is too big to put into a single sentence.

HESTER (*slowly*). Perhaps the answer could be put into a single word.

COLLYER. We might disagree on the choice of that word.

HESTER. I don't expect so. There are polite words and impolite words. They all add up to the same emotion. (*Pointing to a picture.*) That's my latest.

COLLYER. Very nice. What were you angry with Page about?

HESTER. Oh, lots of things. Always the same things.

COLLYER. What?

HESTER. That word we were talking about just now. Shall we call it love? It saves a lot of trouble.

COLLYER. You said just now his feelings for you hadn't changed.

HESTER. They haven't, Bill. They couldn't, you see. Zero minus zero is still zero.

Pause. COLLYER *pushes her away from him to look into her eyes.*

COLLYER. How long have you known this?

HESTER. From the beginning.

COLLYER. But you told me –

HESTER. I don't know what I told you, Bill. If I lied, I'm sorry. You must blame my conventional upbringing. You see I was brought up to think that in a case of this kind it's more proper for it to be the man who does the loving.

Pause.

COLLYER. But how, in the name of reason, could you have gone on loving a man who, by your own confession, can give you nothing in return?

HESTER. Oh, but he can give me something in return, and even does, from time to time.

COLLYER. What?

HESTER. Himself.

COLLYER *stares at her. There is a pause.*

COLLYER. Perhaps you're right, Hester. Perhaps there is no one who can help you.

HESTER (*mockingly*). Except myself, you were going to say.

COLLYER. Yes, I was.

HESTER. I thought you were. (*She turns to the picture.*) It's rather good, I think, don't you?

COLLYER. Yes. Are you selling it?

HESTER. Oh yes, I suppose so – if anyone will buy it.

COLLYER. I'll buy it.

HESTER (*with a hint of anger*). No, you won't.

COLLYER. Why not?

HESTER. Because I don't want you to – that's why not.

COLLYER. Hester – don't be childish. I like that picture and I'm prepared –

HESTER (*angrily*). Please leave the subject. I wanted your opinion – not your money –

There is a knock on the door.

(*Calling.*) Who is that?

MILLER (*off*). Miller.

HESTER (*to* COLLYER). This is the man who looked after me this morning. I'd better let him in.

COLLYER *nods.* HESTER *opens the door.* MILLER *comes in, now dressed, but untidily.*

MILLER. I told you to stay in bed.

HESTER. Thanks to your ministrations, Mr Miller, I feel perfectly all right now. This is Sir William Collyer – Mr Miller.

The men nod to each other. MILLER *stares at* COLLYER *rather curiously.*

MILLER (*turning to* HESTER). Come down to the light. Just let me look. (*He examines her eyes.*) Tongue.

HESTER *extends her tongue.* MILLER *feels her pulse.*

Yes. You have a strong constitution. (*With a slight smile.*) You should live to a ripe old age.

HESTER (*matching his irony*). Barring accidents, of course.

He turns to go. COLLYER *stops him.*

COLLYER. Mr Miller, I'm very grateful to you for all you did for my – for Mrs Page –

MILLER. You needn't be, Sir William. I did very little for Mrs Page.

COLLYER (*bristling a little*). I take it, Mr Miller, that you're not a qualified medical practitioner?

MILLER. You take it quite correctly.

COLLYER. I only ask because a qualified doctor, in a case of this rather delicate kind, is strictly bound by a certain code.

MILLER. Yes, I've heard of it. It's much the same as the English schoolboy's code, isn't it? No sneaking.

COLLYER (*heavily*). I congratulate you on your knowledge of our idioms, Mr Miller.

MILLER. I've spoken no other language since 1938, except for a year in the Isle of Man. Don't worry, Sir William. Or you – Mrs Page. I won't sneak. I left a bottle of antiseptic in your bedroom. May I get it?

HESTER. Please.

He goes into the bedroom.

COLLYER. I don't think I like the look of him. I'm worried.

HESTER. He looks too much like a blackmailer to be one.

COLLYER. I don't share your confidence. Damn it! We ought at least to have offered him a fee –

HESTER. He wouldn't accept it. You'd insult him –

COLLYER. I wonder. It's a fair test.

MILLER *emerges from the bedroom with a bottle in his hand.*

Mr Miller – if you were a qualified practitioner there is one other thing you would do.

MILLER *looks at* COLLYER *inquiringly.* COLLYER *takes out his wallet and pulls out a five-pound note, which he politely extends to* MILLER.

MILLER (*after a pause, with a faint smile*). Thank you. I'll send you a receipt.

He takes the note and goes out. COLLYER *makes an expressive gesture at* HESTER.

HESTER. You win.

COLLYER. The study of human nature is, after all, my profession. If there's any trouble from him, please get in touch with me at once.

HESTER (*wearily*). Yes, Bill.

COLLYER (*looking at his watch*). I must go. I have to be in court in fifteen minutes.

HESTER. Did you bring the car?

COLLYER. Yes.

HESTER. Still the Austin?

COLLYER. No. A new one. Or rather an older one – but a Rolls.

HESTER. Oh, I must have a look at it. (*She goes to the window and peers through. She darts back immediately.*) Oh Lord! You brought Flitton. I wonder who he thought you were going to visit in this low neighbourhood. You didn't tell him?

COLLYER. Of course not.

HESTER. How is he?

COLLYER. Very well.

HESTER. I miss him, you know. I miss them all. Even Miss Wilson. I bet she's been pounding that typewriter with a positive paean of triumph since I left.

COLLYER. There is, perhaps a certain added flourish to her style. (*He points to the picture over the fireplace.*) I do like that picture very much.

HESTER. You shall have it.

Pause.

COLLYER (*quietly*). Thank you very much. What a very handsome present!

HESTER *squeezes his hand gratefully.*

Which reminds me – many happy returns of yesterday.

HESTER. Thank you, Bill – (*Indicating the picture.*) Will you take this now, or shall I send it?

COLLYER (*after a slight pause*). May I call for it?

HESTER. When?

COLLYER. What time are you expecting Page?

HESTER. Not till about seven.

COLLYER. I'll come to tea.

HESTER. About five?

COLLYER. Five-twenty.

HESTER. Right!

COLLYER. Goodbye.

HESTER. Goodbye.

They shake hands, a little shyly.

COLLYER. I wish you'd try to find a way I could help you.

HESTER (*quietly*). I'll try to find a way.

COLLYER *smiles back at her and goes.* HESTER, *left alone, takes a cigarette from her pocket. Then, having lit it, she goes to the window, concealing herself behind the curtains, but looking out. We hear the sound of a car door slam, and of the car drawing away.* HESTER *sighs. Then she goes to the sofa, lies down on it (her back to the door), and picks up a book. After a moment she puts the book down on her lap and stares sightlessly ahead. The door opens and* FREDDIE PAGE *comes in. He is in his late twenties or early thirties, with that sort of boyish good looks that does not indicate age. He carries a suitcase and a bag of golf clubs. The latter he deposits in a corner with a rattle. It is plain that* HESTER *has heard him come in, but she does not turn her head. During the ensuing scene she never looks at him at all, until the moment indicated later.*

FREDDIE. Hullo, Hes. How's tricks? I've just done ninety-three down the Great West. Alvis – smashing job. Jackie Jackson gave me a lift. We gave up the idea of playing golf. It started to rain. It's pouring down at Sunningdale. By the way, a bloody great Rolls was just moving off from here as I came in. I wonder whose it is, do you know?

HESTER, *still staring ahead of her, does not reply.*

Do you think old Elton's lashed out and invested his life savings? Shouldn't be surprised, considering what he must make out of us.

HESTER. Did you have a good weekend?

FREDDIE. Not bad. Won both my matches. I took a fiver off Jackie. Match-bye and bye-bye. He was livid. I wanted to double the stakes – but he wouldn't wear it.

HESTER. How much did you win altogether?

FREDDIE. Seven.

HESTER. Can I have some of it – for Mrs Elton?

FREDDIE. I thought you were going to sell those pictures. Is there any coffee left?

HESTER. I'm not now.

FREDDIE. Why not?

HESTER. I've given one away.

FREDDIE (*mildly*). That was a bloody silly thing to go and do, wasn't it?

HESTER. Yes. I suppose it was.

FREDDIE. Oh hell! All right. You can have three. I need the rest for lunch. I'm taking a South American to the Ritz. Get me giving lunch parties at the Ritz!

HESTER. What South American?

FREDDIE. Bloke I met at golf yesterday. Aircraft business. I got myself given the old intro to him – you know – one of England's most famous test pilots, D.F.C. and bar, D.S.O., all the old ex-Spitfire bull. He seemed impressed.

HESTER. So he should.

FREDDIE. Funny thing about gongs, when you think what a lottery they were. They don't mean a damn thing in war – except as a line-shoot, but in peacetime they're quite useful. This bloke's worth bags of dough. He's got some sort of tie-up with Vickers over here I think. He might fix something.

HESTER. I hope so.

FREDDIE. Anyway he ought to be good for a touch. I say – do you know you haven't looked at me once since I came in?

HESTER. Haven't I, Freddie?

FREDDIE. Why's that?

HESTER. I can remember what you look like.

> FREDDIE *gets up from an armchair where he has been sprawling and goes over to* HESTER.

FREDDIE (*with a guilty look*). I haven't done anything, have I?

HESTER (*smiling*). No, Freddie. You haven't done anything.

FREDDIE. You're not peeved about last night, are you? You see, the blokes wanted to play again today, and if I'd let 'em down –

HESTER. That's all right.

FREDDIE. You were funny on the phone, too, I remember. There wasn't any special reason you wanted me back to dinner last night, was there?

> HESTER, *still not looking at him, does not reply. She gets up from the sofa, her back to him. A sudden thought strikes* FREDDIE.

FREDDIE (*explosively*). Oh my God! (*After an embarrassed pause.*) Many happy returns!

HESTER. Thank you, Freddie.

FREDDIE. Blast! I remembered it on Saturday too. I was going past Barkers' and I thought, it's too late to get her a present now, I'll have to find a shop open on Sunday. Cigarettes, or something. Had you arranged anything special for dinner?

HESTER. Nothing very special. Steak and a bottle of claret.

FREDDIE. We'll have it tonight.

HESTER. Yes.

FREDDIE. Come on now, Hes. No more sulks, please. I've said I'm sorry. I can't say more, can I?

HESTER. No. You can't say more.

FREDDIE (*coaxingly*). Come on, now. Give us a shot of those gorgeous blue orbs. I haven't seen 'em for two whole days –

HESTER turns round and looks at him.

This is me. Freddie Page. Remember?

HESTER. I remember.

He walks forward and kisses her. Instantly she responds, with an intensity of emotion that is almost ugly. After a moment he pushes her away and smacks her playfully.

FREDDIE. Naughty to sulk with your Freddie. Go and get dressed. We'll have a quick one at the Belvedere to celebrate.

HESTER (*at the bedroom door*). Do you want me to lunch with your South American?

FREDDIE. No. Better not. I can shoot a better line without your beady eyes on me.

HESTER. They were gorgeous orbs a moment ago.

FREDDIE. They get beady in company. Go on, darling. Hurry.

HESTER (*who has been staring at him fixedly*). Yes.

FREDDIE (*jocularly*). Still love me?

HESTER (*steadily*). I still love you.

She goes out. After a moment she opens the door again. (Note – it opens inwards.) She is taking off her dressing-gown as she speaks and hanging it up on a hook on the door.

Darling, where are you going to be between five and six?

FREDDIE. Nowhere particularly. Why?

HESTER. Do you mind being out? I've got someone coming in I want to see alone.

FREDDIE. A customer?

HESTER. Yes.

FREDDIE. O.K. I'll go to that new club down the road.

HESTER (*smiling*). And don't get sozzled, either. Remember
our dinner.

FREDDIE. You shut up.

*She disappears, leaving the door open. We can hear bath
water being run. FREDDIE feels in his pocket for a
cigarette, and brings out an empty package.*

(*Calling.*) Darling – I'm out of cigarettes. Have you got any?

HESTER (*off, calling*). There are some in my dressing-gown
pocket.

FREDDIE. Right.

*He goes to the bedroom door and fumbles in the pocket of
HESTER's dressing-gown. He brings out a letter first, and
then the packet. He is about to replace the letter when he
glances at the envelope. He raises his eyebrows, and brings
the letter into the room. Sitting down, he lights a cigarette,
and then tears open the letter, and begins to read.*

HESTER (*off*). Have you got them?

FREDDIE (*his brows knit over the letter, which is a long one*).
What? Yes. I've got them, thanks. (*He continues to read.*)

Curtain.

ACT TWO

*Scene: the same. It is now about five o'clock in the afternoon of
the same day.* FREDDIE *is sprawling, in the attitude in which
we have already seen him, in one armchair, while his friend,*
JACKIE JACKSON, *reclines in another. There is a bottle of
whisky on the table, and a siphon, and both men are holding
glasses.*

FREDDIE (*in an injured tone*). But it's too bloody silly, old boy
   – just because I forgot her birthday.

   JACKIE *makes a sympathetic sound.* FREDDIE *morosely
   takes another gulp of whisky.*

   My God – if all the men who forgot their wives' birthdays
   were to come home and find suicide notes waiting for them,
   the line of widowers would stretch from here to – to John
   o' Groats.

JACKIE. Further, old boy.

FREDDIE. You can't go further.

JACKIE. Well – from here to John o' Groats and back – and
   ending up at the Windmill, then.

FREDDIE (*angrily*). Shut up, Jackie. This isn't funny. I asked
   you round for help and advice and not to let loose a flood of
   corny wisecracks.

JACKIE. Sorry, Freddie, only the way you tell it, it sounds so
   idiotic. Are you sure it wasn't a joke, just to scare you?

FREDDIE. I've told you it wasn't.

   FREDDIE *has risen and is taking* JACKIE'*s glass from his
   willing hand for replenishment.*

JACKIE. Oh – thanks, old chap.

FREDDIE. I got the whole story out of old Ma Elton. She definitely tried to gas herself, and would have succeeded if there'd been a shilling in the blasted meter – (*He has replenished both glasses generously.*)

JACKIE. Well – that shows she couldn't have been too serious about it. (*Taking glass from* FREDDIE.) Oh, thanks. Cheers.

FREDDIE. Where's your imagination? If you're in a state of mind where you're going to try and bump yourself off, you don't think about things like meters.

JACKIE (*judiciously*). Well, I would.

FREDDIE. That from the man who once wrote off three Spits by forgetting to put his ruddy undercart down.

JACKIE. That was different. I wasn't trying to bump myself off.

FREDDIE. You gave a fairly good imitation of it –

JACKIE (*bridling*). At the Court of Inquiry it was definitely established –

FREDDIE. Oh shut up, Jackie. We're talking of something a good deal more important –

JACKIE. Well, you started it. All I said was – about the meter –

FREDDIE. I know what you said about the meter. But you're wrong. I've been into the whole thing, and you can take it from me that she did definitely try, last night, to kill herself.

JACKIE. And all because you forgot her birthday? But that's just the sort of black I'm always putting up with Liz.

FREDDIE. I know. I tell you, Jackie – it knocked me ruddy flat.

JACKIE. I can imagine.

FREDDIE (*explosively*). My God, aren't women the end!

JACKIE (*nodding sympathetically*). Where is she now?

FREDDIE. Out looking for me, I shouldn't wonder. (*He collects* JACKIE*'s glass again.*)

JACKIE. No thanks.

FREDDIE *replenishes his own glass as he speaks.*

FREDDIE. She was having her bath. After I'd read that letter I ran downstairs to Ma Elton and after that I just did a bunk. I had to have a drink quick, and anyway I was damned if I was going in to Hes and fall on my knees and say my darling I have grievously sinned in forgetting your birthday; if I promise you I'll never do it again, will you promise me you'll never gas yourself again. I mean the whole thing's too damn' idiotic –

JACKIE. There must be something else.

FREDDIE. There isn't anything else.

JACKIE (*tentatively*). Another girl?

FREDDIE. There never has been.

JACKIE. Had a lot of rows lately?

FREDDIE. No. As a matter of fact these last few months I've been thinking we've been getting on better than before.

JACKIE (*evidently remembering Liz*). There must have been some rows.

FREDDIE. Very minor ones. Nothing like the real flamers we had when we first started.

JACKIE. What were they about?

FREDDIE (*uncomfortably*). Usual things.

   JACKIE *waits for him to continue.*

   (*Explosively.*) Damn it, Jackie, you know me. I can't be a ruddy Romeo all the time.

JACKIE. Who can?

FREDDIE. According to her the whole damn' human race – male part of it, anyway.

JACKIE. What does she know about it?

FREDDIE. Damn all. A clergyman's daughter, living in Oxford, marries the first man who asks her and falls in love with the first man who gives her an eye. (*After a slight pause.*) Hell, it's not that I'm not in love with her too, of course I am. Always have been and always will. But – well –

moderation in all things – that's always been my motto. (*At the table.*) Have another?

JACKIE. Only a spot.

FREDDIE (*pouring himself one*). I've got nothing on my conscience in that respect. I never gave myself that sort of a build-up with her. She knew what she was taking on.

JACKIE. You don't think it's the marriage question that's upset her?

FREDDIE. No. I'm the one that gets upset by that – not her. Personally I can't wait for that divorce. All this hole-in-the-corner stuff gets me down.

JACKIE. Doesn't it get her down too? I mean – a clergyman's daughter?

FREDDIE. She jumped that fence a year ago. I was the one that wanted to wait. She didn't. That was the first of our flamers. (*He moodily sips his drink, lost in thought.*) My God, it's so damned unfair. Supposing she'd pulled it off last night, do you realize what everyone would have said? That I'd bust up a happy marriage, and then driven Hes to suicide. I'd have been looked on as a ruddy murderer. Did she think of that, I wonder? Who the hell would have believed what I've just told you?

JACKIE (*with unconscious irony*). Anyone who knows you.

FREDDIE. Yes, but this would have been front-page stuff. All over the ruddy *News of the World,* Jackie. Think of that. And this read out in court. (*He flourishes the letter.*) My gosh, I'd have been lucky to have got out without being lynched. The coroner would certainly have added a ruddy rider. I was thinking at lunch today at the Ritz – I'd never have been able to go into any restaurant again, without people nudging and pointing –

JACKIE. Yes, I know. By the way, how did that go off – your lunch with Lopez?

FREDDIE (*savagely*). Do you mind not changing the subject? Or if I'm boring you with this story, just say so and we'll have a little chat about the weather.

JACKIE. I'm sorry. I only wanted to know if he'd offered you anything. That's all. Go on about Hes, then.

FREDDIE (*muttering*). Hell. This is really getting me down. Sorry, Jackie. Didn't mean to bite your head off.

JACKIE. That's all right.

FREDDIE. Lopez? Yes, he offered me a job all right.

JACKIE. Good show.

FREDDIE (*sullenly*). Test pilot – in South America.

JACKIE. Oh Lord! I don't suppose you want to go to South America.

FREDDIE. I don't want to go anywhere – as a test pilot.

JACKIE. They say you were the tops.

FREDDIE. I was – a year ago. Since then things have changed a bit. (*He points to his glass.*) This stuff isn't exactly what the doctor ordered for nerve and judgment. Besides I'm too ruddy old. You're finished in that racket at twenty-five. I wouldn't last a week. I want something chairborne – not airborne. I've had flying for life. (*He rises to get another drink.*) Want one?

JACKIE. No, thanks. Do you think you ought to?

FREDDIE. I know I ought to. Why? Am I drunk?

JACKIE. No. It's only that I gather you've been at it most of the morning.

FREDDIE. And I shall be at it most of the evening too. I shall be at it until I've forgotten that this (*He indicates the letter.*) ever existed.

He gets himself a drink and slumps back into his chair. In speech and in manner he is not drunk, but from now on he is beginning to show some of the wildness and excitability of the habitual drinker who has had about his complement.

JACKIE (*pointing to the letter in* FREDDIE*'s hand*). Doesn't that give you any more clues?

FREDDIE. Read it and see.

JACKIE. No. I don't think so.

FREDDIE. Squeamish, aren't you?

JACKIE. Well – a thing like that – it's a bit – private, isn't it?

FREDDIE. Blasted private, it would have been, read out in court, by the coroner, wouldn't it?

JACKIE. There *is* that, I suppose.

FREDDIE. There *is* that, you suppose. All right. I'm the coroner. You're the public. Now listen. (*Reading.*) 'My darling – a moment ago, before I took the aspirin, I knew exactly what I wanted to say to you. I have run through this letter in my mind so very often and it has always been most eloquent and noble and composed. Now – those moving, pretty words just don't seem to be there. I think that's because, this time, I know I really am going to die.'

JACKIE (*acutely uncomfortable*). Look, old boy, don't go on. Knowing Hes as I do, I'd really rather not hear the rest –

FREDDIE. You're damn well going to hear the rest. I've got to read this to someone.

JACKIE. Still it's addressed to you and no one else.

FREDDIE. No one else – except, of course, the readers of all the Sunday papers. Listen, blast you. (*Reading.*) 'I know that, in the morning, when you read this letter, any feelings you ever had for me, and you had some, will be driven out of your heart for ever. Poor Freddie – poor darling Freddie. I'm so sorry.' (*To* JACKIE, *derisively.*) Sorry! All right. Here's your clue. (*Reading.*) 'You'll want to know why, and I'd so much like to make you understand, because if you understood you might forgive. But to understand what I'm doing now, you must feel even a small part of what I'm feeling now, and that I know you can never do. Just accept that it isn't your fault – it really isn't, Freddie – believe that. You can't help being as you are – I can't help being as I am. The fault lies with whichever of the gods had himself a good laugh up above by arranging for the two of us to meet –

HESTER *comes in quietly.* JACKIE *sees her and signals to* FREDDIE *who does not notice.*

Forgive my bad writing. I think perhaps the drug is beginning – '

HESTER (*in a cool voice*). Hullo, Jackie.

JACKIE. Hullo.

HESTER. How are you?

JACKIE. Very well, thanks, Hes.

HESTER. Where have you two been all afternoon?

JACKIE (*in an agony of embarrassment*). I haven't been with Freddie. I was at home, and he rang up. Asked me over for a chat –

HESTER. I see. (*To* FREDDIE.) Where were you, Freddie?

FREDDIE. A lot of places.

HESTER. I've been to most of them.

FREDDIE. I thought you might.

HESTER. Can I have that letter?

FREDDIE. Why?

HESTER. It belongs to me.

FREDDIE. There might be two views about that. It's got my name on the envelope.

HESTER. An undelivered letter belongs, I should say, to the sender. (*Lightly.*) Please.

HESTER *stands with her hand out, facing* FREDDIE. *He gives her the letter and moves away from her. She tears it up methodically and throws the pieces into the waste-paper-basket. Then she takes the bottle of whisky and goes over to a cupboard.*

FREDDIE. What are you doing?

HESTER. Tidying up.

FREDDIE. It's my bottle. I paid for it. (*He takes it away from her and puts it back on the table.*)

HESTER (*lightly to* JACKIE). Did you have a good game yesterday, Jackie?

JACKIE. Yes, thanks.

HESTER. I hear Freddie beat you. He must be getting rather good.

JACKIE. Off that handicap, he is. It's a crying scandal. Look, Hes – I really think I ought to be dashing along.

HESTER. No, don't go, please. Freddie'll be going out in a minute or two, and I expect he'd like you to go with him. (*To* FREDDIE.) Darling, you hadn't forgotten about being out at five, had you?

FREDDIE. Yes. I had. What's the time now?

HESTER. Getting on. (*She goes to the picture she has given to her husband, and takes it down from the wall.*)

FREDDIE. And of course you don't want your respectable art lover to see me in my present state.

HESTER. I don't know anything about your present state, Freddie. I told you this morning I wanted you to be out.

FREDDIE (*pointing to the picture which she is now holding*). I thought you'd given that away.

HESTER. I have. I'm going to wrap it up.

FREDDIE. Then what are you going to sell this bloke?

HESTER (*at door, with a bright smile*). Whatever he wants to buy.

She goes out with the picture.

FREDDIE (*derisively at the closed door*). Ha! Ha!

JACKIE (*concerned*). Look, Freddie, old boy, I do think you ought to go and talk to her. I'll disappear –

FREDDIE. I've got time enough to talk to her. I've got a whole blasted lifetime to talk to her. You stay. (*He pours himself a drink.*)

JACKIE. Go easy on the Scotch, old boy.

FREDDIE. I've told you. I need it. Delicious oblivion.

JACKIE. Look, Freddie, old boy, I don't want to be rude, but you don't think perhaps, you might be dramatizing this thing a bit too much?

FREDDIE. Dramatizing? She's the one that's dramatizing. That cool, calm, collected act just now – you saw it. That's dramatizing – she enjoys that. I'm just a bloke who's having a couple of drinks because he's feeling ruddy miserable –

JACKIE. I don't expect she can be feeling exactly happy herself – whatever you say about her act just now.

FREDDIE. I suppose if she were Liz and you were in my place, you'd smother her with tender embraces –

JACKIE. I think I'd talk to her about it. I'd ask her what the trouble was, and what I could do to put it right –

FREDDIE. What the hell's the use of that? You heard that letter. Poor Freddie. You can't help being as you are. She's put her finger on it, all right. What am I supposed to do to put that little trouble right? Pretend to be something different? That'd be a lot of help, wouldn't it?

JACKIE. A few white lies –

FREDDIE. Don't be a clot. A few white lies! Dammit, man, talk sense. Do you think she's as easily fooled as that? You seem to see this as the sort of problem that that woman deals with in her advice column in the *Daily Whatsit* – a little domestic tiff that can be put right with a few kind words and a loving peck. Hes tried to kill herself last night.

JACKIE (*murmuring sadly*). I'm sorry, old boy. Perhaps I'm a bit out of my depth.

FREDDIE. Out of your depth? I should bloody well say you are. I'm out of my depth too, and it's a sensation I don't care for. My God, how I hate getting tangled up in other people's emotions. It's the one thing I've tried to avoid all my life, and yet it always seems to be happening to me. Always. (*After a pause.*) You remember Dot during the war, don't you? I brought her down to the squadron a couple of times?

JACKIE. Yes. I liked her a lot. A load of fun –

FREDDIE. A load of fun, until she started messing about with my service revolver.

JACKIE. She didn't –

FREDDIE. No. She didn't hurt herself or me or anyone else. Still you can imagine that the fun got a bit sour after that. And then there was – (*He stops.*) It doesn't matter. Too many emotions. Far too ruddy many. I loathe 'em.

JACKIE. A sort of *homme fatal,* eh?

FREDDIE (*quietly*). It's not so funny, you know, Jackie. It's not so funny. Hes says I've got no feelings and perhaps she's right, but anyway I've got something inside that can get hurt – the way it's hurt now. I don't enjoy causing other people misery. I'm not a ruddy sadist. My sort never gets a hearing. We're called a lot of rude names, and nobody ever thinks we have a case. But look at it this way, Jackie. Take two people – 'A' and 'B'. 'A' loves 'B' – 'B' doesn't love 'A', or at least not in the same way. He wants to, but he just can't. It's not his nature. Now 'B' hasn't asked to be loved. He may be a perfectly ordinary bloke, kind, well-meaning, good friend, perhaps even a good husband if he's allowed to be. But he's not allowed to be – that's my point. Demands are made on him which he just can't fulfil. If he tries, he's cheating, and cheating doesn't help anyone. Now if he's honest and doesn't try – well, then everyone says he's a skunk and a heartless cad, and coroners add ruddy riders. I mean – where are you? (*He finishes his drink.*) Come on. We'd better get weaving.

He goes to collect his coat. There is a knock on the door. FREDDIE *goes to open it.* MILLER *is outside.*

MILLER. Excuse me. Is Mrs Page in?

FREDDIE. No, not at the moment. You're Mr Miller, aren't you?

MILLER. Yes. And you are Mr Page?

FREDDIE. That's right. Come in. I want to talk to you.

MILLER. Thank you.

FREDDIE. You looked after my wife, this morning, didn't you?

MILLER. Yes. I looked after Mrs Page.

FREDDIE (*introducing*). This is Jackie Jackson. Mr Miller.

The two men nod to each other.

(*To* MILLER.) Care for a drink?

MILLER. Thank you.

FREDDIE. I'd like to know how much she said to you. Mrs Elton says you were with her alone. (*Indicating* JACKIE.) You needn't worry about him. He knows all about it.

MILLER. She said nothing.

FREDDIE. Nothing about why she did it?

MILLER. Nothing.

FREDDIE *hands him a drink.*

FREDDIE. Do you know why she did it?

MILLER. No.

FREDDIE. If you like I'll tell you.

JACKIE (*interposing*). No, Freddie –

FREDDIE. She did it because I forgot her birthday.

MILLER. Yes.

FREDDIE. You don't look surprised.

MILLER. I'm not. I assumed it was something of the kind.

FREDDIE. Something so trivial?

MILLER. Nothing can be called trivial that induces an operative desire to die.

FREDDIE. But forgetting a birthday –

MILLER. Yes. That is trivial.

FREDDIE. A riddler – this bloke. All right. What's the real reason, then? What's behind the triviality?

MILLER. I don't think you need me to tell you that.

FREDDIE. I'd like to hear it, anyway.

MILLER. Yourself, I should suppose.

FREDDIE. Which just about makes me a ruddy murderer.

MILLER (*politely*). A ruddy near-murderer.

JACKIE (*interposing*). Look – I don't think you ought to say a
    thing like –

FREDDIE. Shut up, Jackie. I can take it.

JACKIE. But he doesn't know the facts –

FREDDIE. The facts? What the hell do the facts matter?
    It's what's behind the facts that matters, isn't that so,
    Mr Miller?

MILLER. Yes.

FREDDIE. And what's behind the facts is me.

MILLER. I imagine so.

FREDDIE. Little murdering me.

    MILLER *nods.*

    All right, my friend, and what would you do about it if you
    were me?

MILLER. That's a stupid question. Nature has not endowed me
    with the capacity for inspiring suicidal love.

FREDDIE. Aren't you lucky?

MILLER. Yes, I suppose I am.

FREDDIE. And what about a poor bloke who has this capacity
    for inspiring suicidal love – what does *he* do about it?

MILLER. Refuse to love at all, I'd say.

    There is a pause. FREDDIE *turns to the bottle of whisky.*

FREDDIE. Have another drink. My God – we've had this bottle.
    (*He is pouring the last few drops into* MILLER*'s glass.*)

MILLER. Thank you.

FREDDIE. What you've just said, old boy, was a load of tripe.

MILLER. Very possibly. As this gentleman has already pointed out, I know nothing of the facts.

FREDDIE. One of the facts is that this character has no intention, at this stage in his life, of turning himself into a bloody hermit.

MILLER. No. I imagine he hasn't.

FREDDIE. You're damn' right, he hasn't, old boy. Look – let's continue this argument down the road. That new club opens at four.

JACKIE. Look, Freddie, I think I ought to be getting along. Liz'll be wondering –

FREDDIE (*ironically*). Liz'll be wondering. (*Waving at JACKIE.*) Portrait of a happily married man, Mr Miller. A man who can be fairly certain of coming home and not finding his loving wife lying in front of a gas-fire –

HESTER comes in, the picture now neatly wrapped and tied. She puts it away in a corner.

HESTER (*to* MILLER). Oh hullo.

MILLER. Good afternoon.

JACKIE. I was just on my way, Hes.

HESTER. Must you go?

JACKIE. I must, I'm afraid. You're turning us out of the flat anyway, aren't you?

HESTER (*pleadingly*). Yes. But I hoped you'd keep Freddie company.

JACKIE. I'm afraid I can't, Hes. I've got people coming in.

FREDDIE. Bad luck, darling. No nurse for poor little Freddie-weddie –

He is putting on his coat, with slight difficulty. MILLER *helps him.*

Unless, of course, Mr Miller here would like to volunteer for the job.

MILLER. I'm afraid I have some work to do.

FREDDIE. Work? What sort of work? Curing other people's love problems?

MILLER. No. Sending out a list of the latest prices for the St. Leger.

FREDDIE. You a bookie?

MILLER. Yes.

FREDDIE. I should never have thought it. What price is Makeshift?

MILLER. A hundred to seven.

FREDDIE. I'll have fifty to three-ten. That's to say if you'll accept me as a client –

MILLER *takes out a notebook and makes a note.*

MILLER. I'll submit your name to my proprietor.

FREDDIE. That's not you?

MILLER. Oh no. I'm only one of his many assistants.

JACKIE (*at the door*). Well, cheerio, Freddie. (*To* MILLER.) Goodbye.

HESTER. Give my love to Liz.

FREDDIE. You'd better not give her *my* love, Jackie. From all accounts it's pretty lethal.

JACKIE. Goodbye.

HESTER (*to* JACKIE). Goodbye.

JACKIE *goes.*

HESTER *waits at the door for* FREDDIE. *On his way there he stops at the table, picks up the bottle, and deposits it in the waste-paper basket.*

FREDDIE. Just tidying up. (*He walks on to the door.*)

HESTER (*trying to conceal her anxiety*). Freddie – I don't know that you should go out, you know.

FREDDIE. I thought you wanted me out. Your customer –

HESTER. Mrs Elton can give him a message. He can come back some other time. Why don't you go and have a good lie down?

FREDDIE. No. I'm a good boy. When I'm told to go – I go – (*He fumbles in his pockets. To* MILLER.) Can you lend me a shilling?

MILLER *produces a shilling and gives it to him.* FREDDIE *throws it on to the table.*

Just in case I'm late for dinner.

He goes out. HESTER *goes out on to the landing and watches him go down the stairs. Though drunk his legs are (and have been through the previous scene) supporting him fairly steadily.* HESTER *turns back into the room.*

HESTER (*urgently*). Do you know where he's going?

MILLER. To the new club down the road.

HESTER. Are you really working, or was that just an excuse?

MILLER. I'm really working.

HESTER. Oh. (*She moves anxiously to the window.*)

MILLER. He'll be happier by himself than with me, you know.

HESTER. Why do you say that?

MILLER. Because I seem to have become the embodiment of his conscience.

HESTER (*bitterly*). His conscience? You appear to have found something in him that I've missed.

MILLER. They say the eyes of love are blind.

HESTER. They say that about the loved one's failings – not about his virtues. And my eyes aren't blind. They can see, quite well.

MILLER. I know they can. Too well.

HESTER *looks at him.*

To love with one's eyes open sometimes makes life very difficult.

HESTER. Even – unbearable.

MILLER. I said – difficult.

HESTER. I don't like him being alone.

MILLER. Very well. I shall volunteer.

HESTER. Thank you very much, Mr Miller. I'm very grateful.

MILLER. There's no need. (*Pointing to a picture.*) Did you paint that?

HESTER. Yes.

MILLER. I only ask because it doesn't seem to be at all in the style of the others.

HESTER. I was seventeen when I did that.

MILLER. Indeed. (*He examines it.*) Interesting. Did you go to Art School?

HESTER. No.

MILLER. There is a delicacy and freshness about this which is very striking.

HESTER. Hurry to Freddie, please. I'm very anxious.

There is a knock on the door. HESTER goes to it and opens it. COLLYER is on the threshold. He comes in.

You're early.

COLLYER. I know. I came straight from court.

MILLER. I'm just going, Sir William. I have an errand to perform for – Mrs Page. Oh, by the way – I was going to put this in the post.

He takes an envelope from his pocket and hands it to COLLYER. He goes out.

HESTER. I ought to have asked you to phone me. Freddie came back unexpectedly and has only just gone out. (*Indicating envelope.*) What's that? Your receipt?

COLLYER. I imagine so. (*He opens the envelope and takes out a five-pound note.*) This is a piece of insolence. He's written on the back: 'For quasi-professional services, received with thanks. K. Miller.'

HESTER *smiles as* COLLYER *puts the note back in his case.*

Yes. I suppose the laugh is on me. What was this errand he was talking about?

HESTER. It doesn't matter. I promised you tea, didn't I?

COLLYER. Don't bother about tea. Moments are precious. I don't want you to waste them over a kettle in the kitchen. It's all right for me to stay for a moment or two, isn't it?

HESTER. Yes, Bill, I think so.

COLLYER. I saw Page just now.

HESTER. Did he see you?

COLLYER. No. I was in the car, just turning into this street. I put a newspaper up. He couldn't possibly have seen me. Besides he was quite obviously drunk.

HESTER. Oh? What makes you think that?

COLLYER. His passage down the street was rather erratic.

HESTER (*brightly*). I don't think it could have been Freddie you saw, Bill. He only left this flat a moment ago –

COLLYER (*reproachfully*). Hester – (*He indicates the glasses on the table.*)

HESTER. He'd been having a drink with a friend.

COLLYER *picks out of the waste-paper basket the empty bottle, the head of which is showing.*

HESTER (*angrily*). Really, Bill. Even a judge can let his imagination run away with him. (*She takes the bottle and puts it away in a cupboard.*)

COLLYER. How long has it been going on?

HESTER. How long has what been going on?

COLLYER. In the old days he hardly touched alcohol.

HESTER (*shortly*). Is that so? I don't remember.

COLLYER. Of course you remember. He never drank at Sunningdale. He used to say it was bad for his judgment as a pilot.

HESTER (*quietly*). Very well, then, Bill. If in the last ten months Freddie's taken to drink, it must be I who've driven him to it.

COLLYER (*equally quietly*). And he who's driven you to suicide.

HESTER. No. I drove myself there.

Pause.

COLLYER. Hester, what's happened to you?

HESTER. Love, Bill, that's all – you know – that thing you read about in your beloved Jane Austen and Anthony Trollope. Love. 'It droppeth as the gentle dew from heaven.' No. That's wrong, isn't it? I know. 'It comforteth like sunshine after rain – '

COLLYER. Rather an unfortunate quotation. Go on with it.

HESTER. I can't. I've forgotten.

COLLYER. 'Love comforteth like sunshine after rain and Lust's effect is tempest after sun.'

HESTER. Tempest after sun? That would be very apt, wouldn't it, if that were all I felt for Freddie.

COLLYER. In sober truth, Hester, isn't it?

HESTER (*angrily*). Oh, God, Bill, do you really think I can tell you the sober truth about what I feel for Freddie? I've got quite a clear mind – too clear, I've just been told – and if it were only my *mind* that were involved . . . But in sober truth, Bill – in sober truth neither you nor I nor anyone else can explain what I feel for Freddie. It's all far too big and confusing to be tied up in such a neat little parcel and labelled lust. Lust isn't the whole of life – and Freddie is, you see, to me. The whole of life – and of death, too, it seems. Put a label on that, if you can – (*She turns abruptly.*) Gosh! I wish Freddie hadn't drunk all the whisky.

COLLYER. Would you like to go out?

HESTER. No. I'd better stay in and await developments.

COLLYER. What developments?

HESTER. Oh – quite a large variety are apt to offer themselves when Freddie's on the rampage –

She sits down, facing away from COLLYER. *There is a pause while he stares at her.*

COLLYER (*at length*). What made us choose Sunningdale that summer?

HESTER (*at the window*). It was your idea. You wanted the golf.

COLLYER. You weren't keen, I remember. You'd have preferred the sea.

HESTER (*absently*). Yes.

Pause.

COLLYER. You know you never told me exactly how it first happened.

HESTER. No. I suppose I didn't.

There is a pause before she begins. While she speaks she does not look at COLLYER. *It is almost as though she were talking to herself.*

It was the day you were playing for the President's Cup.

COLLYER. Oh yes, I remember.

HESTER. I came up to the golf club to collect you to go on to that party at the Hendersons'. You were still out playing. Freddie was there alone. He'd been chucked for a game and was bad-tempered. I'd met him several times before up at the club with the others – but I'd never paid much attention to him. I didn't think he was even particularly good-looking, and the R.A.F. slang used to irritate me slightly I remember. It's such an anachronism now, isn't it – as dated as gadzooks and odds my life.

COLLYER. He does it for effect, I suppose.

HESTER. No. He does it because his life stopped in 1940. He loved 1940, you know. There were some like that. He's never been really happy since he left the R.A.F. (*After a slight pause.*) Well – that day you were a long time over your game.

COLLYER. Yes. We were held up badly, I remember.

HESTER. And Freddie and I sat on the veranda together for at least an hour. For some reason he talked very honestly and rather touchingly about himself – how worried he was about his future, how his life seemed to have no direction or purpose, how he envied you – the brilliant lawyer –

COLLYER. That was good of him.

HESTER. He meant it sincerely. Then quite suddenly he put his hand on my arm and murmured something very conventional, about envying you for other reasons besides your career. I laughed at him and he laughed back, like a guilty small boy. He said, 'I really do, you know, it's not just a line. I really think you're the most attractive girl I've ever met.' Something like that. I didn't really listen to the words, because anyway I knew then in that tiny moment when we were laughing together so close that I had no hope. No hope at all.

Pause.

COLLYER. It was that night that you insisted on coming up to London with me, wasn't it?

HESTER. Yes.

COLLYER. You didn't want to come back to Sunningdale the next weekend either, I remember –

HESTER. No.

COLLYER. When, exactly –

HESTER. It was in September. Do you remember I went up to London with him to see a play?

COLLYER. But that meeting in the clubhouse was in June.

HESTER. June the twenty-fourth.

COLLYER (*quietly*). During those two months, why didn't you talk to me about it?

HESTER. What would you have said to me if I had?

COLLYER. What I say now. That this man you say you love is morally and intellectually a mile your inferior and has absolutely nothing in common with you whatever; that what you're suffering from is no more than an ordinary and rather sordid infatuation; and that it's your plain and simple duty to exert every effort of will you're capable of in order to return to sanity at once.

HESTER *nods quietly. There is a pause.*

And how would you have answered that?

HESTER. By agreeing with you, I suppose. But it wouldn't have made any difference. (*She looks at her watch.*)

COLLYER (*at length*). If we'd been able to have a child, how much difference would it have made?

HESTER (*after a pause*). Isn't reality enough to occupy us, Bill?

COLLYER. Meaning, I suppose, that it would have made no difference at all?

HESTER. That's not what I said.

COLLYER. It's fantastic to think what was caused by my decision to rent that damn villa.

HESTER. Don't distress yourself with that sort of thought, Bill. Freddie and I would have met anyway. I think it's time you went.

COLLYER (*ironically*). You believe in affinities?

HESTER (*simply*). I believe it was fated that Freddie and I should meet.

COLLYER. As it's turned out, a pretty evil fate.

HESTER. If there are good affinities there must be evil ones too, I suppose. Don't forget your present, after all the trouble I've been to wrapping it up.

She goes to the parcel and picks it up. A key is suddenly turned in the door and it is thrown open, revealing FREDDIE. *He stands for a time in the doorway, looking from* COLLYER *to* HESTER. *Then he comes in and closes the door behind him. He appears to have sobered up a little.*

FREDDIE. I thought it might be. Not many people who come to this place have a big black Rolls.

HESTER. Where's Miller?

FREDDIE. Miller?

HESTER. Didn't you see him at the club?

FREDDIE. I never went to the club. (*To* COLLYER.) That's the same chauffeur, isn't it?

COLLYER. Yes.

HESTER. Bill came to see me because someone telephoned to him about my accident.

FREDDIE. Yes. (*To* COLLYER.) You've heard about her – accident, have you?

COLLYER. Yes.

FREDDIE. Did you ever forget her birthday?

COLLYER. No.

FREDDIE. No. I shouldn't think you were a forgetful type. You're a judge now, aren't you?

COLLYER. Yes.

FREDDIE. Still making packets of money?

COLLYER. A certain amount.

FREDDIE. Still love Hes?

HESTER (*sharply*). Don't listen to him, Bill. He's drunk. Freddie, you'd better go and lie down.

FREDDIE. See how I'm bullied? I bet you were never bullied like that.

HESTER. Freddie, please try and behave yourself.

FREDDIE. Am I behaving badly? I'm only asking the judge here a simple question. I'd rather like to know the answer. Still, I suppose it doesn't really matter –

He goes into the bedroom, and we hear the door bolted.

HESTER. I'm sorry, Bill.

COLLYER. That's all right.

HESTER. I think perhaps you'd better go.

COLLYER. Yes.

He moves towards his hat and coat, picks them up, and then hesitates uncertainly. HESTER *is not looking at him, but at the bedroom door.*

The answer to that question is yes, you know.

HESTER (*not having understood*). What?

COLLYER. The question Page asked me just now. The answer is yes.

Pause.

HESTER. Bill – please don't –

COLLYER. I'm sorry. (*Indicating bedroom.*) Sure you can cope with the – situation?

HESTER. Oh heavens, yes. This is nothing.

COLLYER. He's changed a lot. He looks quite different.

HESTER. He hasn't been well lately.

COLLYER. No. (*He stretches out his hand.*) Well, goodbye.

HESTER. I'm sorry, Bill. I'm so sorry. Is there anything more I can say?

COLLYER. I don't think so.

He smiles at her. HESTER *kisses him suddenly on the cheek.*

HESTER. Goodbye, Bill.

COLLYER *smiles at her again and goes.* HESTER *closes the door behind him and then goes quickly to the bedroom door. She knocks.*

HESTER (*calling*). Freddie, let me in, darling.

There is no answer. She knocks again.

Freddie – don't be childish. Let me in.

There is no answer. HESTER *walks away from the door and goes to get a cigarette. As she is lighting it* FREDDIE *emerges from the bedroom. He has changed into a blue suit.*

Why, Freddie, you're looking very smart. Going out somewhere?

FREDDIE. Yes.

HESTER. Where?

FREDDIE. To see a man about a job.

HESTER. What man?

FREDDIE. Lopez. I've just called him.

HESTER. Lopez?

FREDDIE. The South American I had lunch with.

HESTER. Oh yes, of course. I'd forgotten. How did it go off?

FREDDIE. It went off all right.

HESTER. Oh good. You think you'll get the job?

FREDDIE. Yes, I think so. He made a fairly definite offer. Of course it's up to his boss.

HESTER. Let's have a look at you. (*She inspects him.*) Oh, darling, you might have changed your shirt.

FREDDIE. Well, I hadn't a clean one.

HESTER. No. Nor you had. The laundry's late again this week. I'll wash one out for you tomorrow.

FREDDIE. Yes. Does it look too bad?

HESTER. No. It'll pass. Your shoes need a clean.

FREDDIE. Yes. I'll give them a rub.

HESTER. No. Take them off. I'll do them. (*She goes towards the kitchen.*) Somehow or other you always manage to get shoe polish over your face – Lord knows how.

She disappears into the kitchen. FREDDIE *takes his shoes off.* HESTER *comes back with shoe brushes and a tin of polish. She takes the shoes from him and begins to clean them. There is a fairly long silence.*

What's the job?

FREDDIE (*muttering*). Yes. I suppose I must tell you.

HESTER *gives him a quick glance.*

HESTER. Yes, Freddie. I think I'd like to know.

FREDDIE. Look, Hes. I've got to talk for a bit now. It's not going to be easy, so don't interrupt, do you mind? You always could argue the hind leg off a donkey – and just when I've got things clear in my mind I don't want them muddled up again.

HESTER. I'm sorry, Freddie. I must interrupt at once. The way you've been behaving this afternoon, how could you have things clear in your mind?

FREDDIE. I'm all right now, Hes. I had a cup of black coffee and after that a bit of a walk. I know what I'm doing.

HESTER. And what are you doing, Freddie?

FREDDIE. Accepting a job in South America as a test pilot.

HESTER. Test pilot? But you've said a hundred times you could never go back to that. After that crash in Canada you told me you had no nerve or judgment left.

FREDDIE. They'll come back. I had too many drinks that time in Canada. You know that.

HESTER. Yes, I know that. So did the Court of Inquiry know that. Does this man Lopez know that?

FREDDIE. No, of course not. He won't hear either. Don't worry about my nerve and judgment, Hes. A month or two on the wagon and I'll be the old ace again – the old dicer with death.

HESTER (*sharply*). Don't use that idiotic R.A.F. slang, Freddie. (*More gently.*) Do you mind? This is too important –

FREDDIE. Yes. It is important.

HESTER. Whereabouts in South America?

FREDDIE. Somewhere near Rio.

HESTER. I see. (*She continues to clean the shoes mechanically.*) Well, when do we start?

FREDDIE. We don't.

HESTER. We don't?

FREDDIE. You and I don't. That's what I'm trying to tell you. I'm going alone.

HESTER *lays the shoe down quietly, staring at* FREDDIE.

HESTER (*at length*) Why, Freddie?

FREDDIE. If I'm to stay on the wagon, I've got to be alone.

HESTER (*in a near whisper*). Have you?

FREDDIE. Oh hell – that's not the real reason. Listen, Hes, darling.

There is a pause while he paces the room as if concentrating desperately on finding the words. HESTER *watches him.*

You've always said, haven't you, that I don't really love you? Well, I suppose, in your sense I don't. But what I do feel for you is a good deal stronger than I've ever felt for anybody else in my life, or ever will feel, I should think. That's why I went away with you in the first place, that's why I've stayed with you all this time, and that's why I must go away from you now.

HESTER (*at length*). That sounds rather like a prepared speech, Freddie.

FREDDIE. Yes. I suppose it is. I worked it out on my walk. But it's still true, Hes. I'm too fond of you to let things slide. That letter was a hell of a shock. I knew often you were unhappy – you often knew I was a bit down too. But I hadn't a clue how much the – difference in our feelings had been hurting you. It's asking too damn' much of any bloke to go on as if nothing had happened when he knows now for a fact that he's driving the only girl he's ever loved to suicide.

HESTER (*in a low voice*). Do you think your leaving me will drive me away from suicide?

FREDDIE (*simply*). That's a risk I shall just have to take, isn't it? It's a risk both of us will have to face.

Pause.

HESTER. Freddie – you mustn't scare me like this.

FREDDIE. No scare, Hes. Sorry, this is on the level.

HESTER. You know perfectly well you'll feel quite differently in the morning.

FREDDIE. No, I won't, Hes. Not this time. Besides I don't think I'll be here in the morning.

HESTER. Where will you be?

FREDDIE. I don't know. Somewhere. I think I'd better get out tonight.

HESTER. No, Freddie. No.

FREDDIE. It's better that way. I'm scared of your arguing. (*Passionately*). I know this is right, you see. I know it, but with your gift of the gab, you'll muddle things up for me again, and I'll be lost.

HESTER. I won't Freddie. I won't. I promise I won't. But you must stay tonight. just tonight.

FREDDIE (*unhappily*). No, Hes.

HESTER. Just tonight, Freddie. Only one night.

FREDDIE. No. Sorry, Hes.

HESTER. Don't be so cruel, Freddie. How can you be so cruel?

FREDDIE. Hes – this is our last chance. If we miss it, we're done for. We're death to each other, you and I.

HESTER. That isn't true.

FREDDIE. It is true, darling, and you've known it longer than I have. I'm such a damn' fool and that's been the trouble, or I should have done this long ago. That's it, you know. It's written in great bloody letters of fire over our heads – 'You and I are death to each other.'

HESTER *is unrestrainedly weeping.* FREDDIE *comes over to her and picks up his shoes.*

HESTER. I haven't finished them.

FREDDIE. They're all right. (*He begins to put them on.*) I'm sorry, Hes. Oh God, I'm sorry. Please don't cry. You don't know what it does to me.

HESTER. Not now. Not this minute. Not this minute, Freddie?

FREDDIE *finishes putting on his shoes, and then turns away from her, brushing his sleeve across his eyes.*

HESTER (*going to him*). You've got all your things here. You've got to pack –

FREDDIE. I'll send for them.

HESTER. You promised to come back for dinner.

FREDDIE. I know. I'm sorry about that. (*He kisses her quickly and goes to the door.*)

HESTER (*frantically*). But you can't break a promise like that, Freddie. You can't. Come back just for our dinner, Freddie. I won't argue, I swear, and then if you want to go away afterwards –

FREDDIE *goes out.* HESTER *runs to the door after him.*

Freddie, come back. . . . Don't go. . . . Don't leave me alone tonight . . . Not tonight . . . Don't leave me alone tonight . . .

She has followed him out as the curtain falls.

ACT THREE

Scene: the same.

At the rise of the curtain HESTER *is sitting, motionless and tense, staring unblinkingly at some object straight ahead of her. After an appreciable pause the telephone rings.* HESTER's *reaction is indicative of the nervous tension which she is undergoing. She reaches for the receiver, then drops her hand, and, standing close to the telephone, allows it to ring for a few times before she takes the receiver off.*

HESTER. Hullo? . . . Oh. No, he's not in, I'm afraid . . . Yes, it is. Who is that? . . . Oh. Yes. Good evening . . . I don't know exactly when he'll be back. What's the time now? . . . Eleven ten? Is it as late as that? . . . Oh no. I wasn't asleep – just reading. . . . Yes, I expect him in quite soon. . . . It's about golf? Yes, I'll get him to ring you. He knows your number, doesn't he? . . . Quite all right. Good night.

She replaces the receiver and now stands for a little time staring at it. After a moment impulsively she puts her hand out to take the receiver, stops – with her hand still outstretched – then drops it hopelessly. She turns away from it, and walks back to her chair, resuming exactly the same pose in which we first discovered her. There is a knock on the door. HESTER *opens it.* MRS ELTON *is outside.*

MRS ELTON. Hullo, dear.

HESTER. Yes, Mrs Elton?

MRS ELTON. Just thought I'd pop up and see how you were. (*Looking round.*) Mr Page not in?

HESTER. No.

MRS ELTON. Don't you want the fire on? It's turned quite cold all of a sudden.

HESTER. No, thank you.

MRS ELTON. Fancy not drawing the curtains.

There is a knock on the half-opened door and ANN WELCH *puts a tentative head round the door.*

ANN. Oh. Excuse me.

HESTER. Good evening.

ANN. Good evening, Mrs Page. I just wondered if Philip was here, by any chance –

HESTER. Philip? Oh, your husband. No. Why should he be?

ANN. I thought perhaps Mr Page was back and –

HESTER (*excitedly*). Is he with him?

ANN. Yes, I think so.

HESTER. Where?

ANN. Well, I don't know. I didn't want to go with them because I had some work to do. Still, they've been gone nearly two hours now and –

HESTER (*to* ANN). How did you meet him?

ANN. We were having our dinner at the Belvedere – and Mr Page was in the bar and then he came up and sat at our table.

HESTER. I see.

ANN. Of course we hardly know him at all, you know, but he was very nice and friendly and said he wanted company, and he gave us a brandy each, and then, after that, he asked Philip to go on with him to this new club for a few moments.

HESTER. Which new club?

ANN. I'm afraid I can't remember the name.

HESTER. How was he?

ANN. Do you mean was he – ?

HESTER. Drunk, yes.

ANN. Well, I wouldn't actually say drunk. Of course that was two hours ago. Philip doesn't drink at all, of course, so that's all right. The only thing is . . . I know it's awfully silly of me . . . but I'm not very good at being left alone.

HESTER (*with a faint smile*). Yes, Mrs Welch. I understand. Well, you mustn't worry. I expect your husband will be back very soon.

ANN. Oh yes. I expect so. If he comes in here, send him straight up, won't you?

HESTER. I will. Good night.

ANN. Good night.

She goes.

HESTER. Mrs Elton, do you remember the name of the new club?

MRS ELTON. No, dear. I don't, I'm afraid.

HESTER. I remember a card came – (*Suddenly.*) The Crow's Nest!

She goes quickly to the telephone book, and begins to search.

MRS ELTON. That's right. I knew it was something like that.

She watches HESTER *sympathetically as she finds the number and begins to dial.*

HESTER. Hullo? . . . Oh, tell me, is Mr Page there? . . . Mr Page . . . Yes, that's right . . . Yes. Oh. How long ago? . . . Half an hour. I see. Do you know where he went? No. It doesn't matter . . . If he comes in again tell him his wife called – (*Frantically.*) no, hold on – waiter – don't tell him anything – anything at all . . . Yes, that's right. Good night.

She rings off. MRS ELTON *shakes her head.*

MRS ELTON. I can't understand how he could go and do a thing like that – leaving you alone tonight after what happened –

HESTER (*abruptly*). Mrs Elton – haven't you got work to do?

MRS ELTON (*quietly*). Yes, dear. Plenty. (*She goes to the door.*)

HESTER (*quickly*). I'm sorry. I didn't mean to be unkind.

MRS ELTON (*turning*). Oh, you don't need to tell me. You couldn't mean to be unkind. You're not that sort. I'll let you into a little secret. You're my favourite tenant.

HESTER. Am I?

MRS ELTON (*nodding*). Sad, isn't it, how one always seems to prefer nice people to good people, don't you think?

She has opened the door. MILLER, wearing an overcoat, is outside. He is carrying a rather large leather bag.

Oh, good evening, Mr Miller. You're back from your work early.

MILLER. Yes. (*To HESTER.*) How are you tonight, Mrs Page?

HESTER. Quite well, thank you. Do you usually work as late as this?

MILLER. Sometimes.

HESTER. What have you got in that formidable looking bag?

MILLER. It is nothing. Nothing at all. (*He turns to go on up the stairs.*)

MRS ELTON. Oh, Mr Miller, I don't like to ask you but I wonder if you'd just have a look at Mr Elton tonight. He's bad again.

MILLER. I'll come down in five minutes.

MRS ELTON. Thank you ever so much. I'm very grateful.

He goes on up the stairs.

You shouldn't have asked him that about the bag, dear. He hates to tell.

HESTER (*abstractedly*). I'm sorry. I wasn't really curious. Just talking for the sake of talking. (*She is staring at the telephone.*)

MRS ELTON. If I were you, dear, I wouldn't use that thing again tonight.

HESTER. Perhaps you're right. (*She sits down.*)

MRS ELTON. Why not go to bed? I'll bring you a nice warm drink –

HESTER *shakes her head.*

Or I'll get Dr. Miller to give you one of his sleeping pills –

HESTER. He *is* a doctor, of course, isn't he?

MRS ELTON. Well. He was.

HESTER. I see. I knew he'd been in trouble.

MRS ELTON. How, dear?

HESTER. Fellow-feeling, I suppose.

MRS ELTON. Yes, he *was* in trouble once. Bad trouble.

HESTER *nods.*

Don't say I told you, will you? Poor Mr Miller! I'm sorry for him. So ashamed of people knowing –

HESTER. Did he tell you about it?

MRS ELTON. No, dear. Just after he'd come here there was a letter for him addressed to 'Kurt Miller, M.D.' – and then of course I remembered the case, because there'd been quite a lot in the papers about it. Of course I didn't let on to him I knew, but he guessed I did all right, because one day when I was saying how tidy he always kept his room, 'Well,' he said, 'Mrs Elton, I suppose tidiness is the only lesson I ever did learn in jail.' Just like that. That was the only time he ever mentioned it, but it was quite soon after that he volunteered to look after Mr Elton. I think it's a wicked shame the way they've treated him. Imagine a man like that being a bookmaker's clerk. There's waste for you, if you like.

HESTER. Why did he take the job?

MRS ELTON. Because beggars can't be choosers, dear, and if a patient of his that was a bookie takes pity on him – well, he's got to eat, hasn't he? Anyway I can tell you what's in that bag if you really want to know. He goes and works every night in a hospital for infantile paralysis – unpaid, of course. That was his speciality before – apparently he was working on some sort of treatment –

HESTER. Won't he ever get back on the Medical Register?

MRS ELTON. Oh no. Not a hope, I should say, dear. You know what they're like, and what he did wasn't – well – the sort of thing people forgive very easily. Ordinary normal people, I mean.

HESTER. You've forgiven it, Mrs Elton.

MRS ELTON. Oh well, I see far too much of life in this place to get upset by that sort of thing. It takes all sorts to make a world, after all – doesn't it? There was a couple once in Number Eleven – (*She stops suddenly.*) I can hear him on the stairs.

She opens the door. MILLER *is descending the stairs.*

I'll go down and get Mr Elton ready, shall I?

MILLER. Yes.

MRS ELTON. I wonder if you'd be kind enough to give Mrs Page one of your sleeping pills.

MILLER. I'd thought of that myself.

MRS ELTON. Good. (*To* HESTER.) Well, good night, dear. If you want anything just give me a ring. I'll be up with Mr Elton most of the night anyway.

She goes. MILLER *comes into the room, takes a bottle from his pocket, and shakes out two pills which he hands to* HESTER.

HESTER. Thank you, Doctor. (*She puts them down on the table.*)

MILLER. I've asked you before not to call me that.

HESTER. I keep forgetting. I'm sorry.

MILLER. Are you going to bed now?

HESTER. In a moment.

MILLER (*turning to go*). Don't let that moment be too long.

HESTER. Everyone is very solicitous of me this evening.

MILLER. Are you surprised? Voices carry on the stairs of this house.

HESTER. Freddie's and mine?

MILLER *nods*.

Everyone heard us, I suppose. All the respectable tenants nudging each other and saying there's that woman's drunken boy friend walking out on her. Serve her right.

MILLER. I didn't say that. But then, of course, I may not be a respectable tenant.

HESTER (*simply*). What should I do?

MILLER. What makes you think I can tell you?

HESTER. How near did *you* come to the gas-fire, once?

Pause. MILLER *turns abruptly away from her.*

MILLER. Mrs Elton, eh? (*He turns back to face her. Abruptly.*) You ask my advice. Take those pills and sleep tonight. In the morning – go on living.

There is a knock on the door. HESTER *opens it.* COLLYER *is outside, dressed in a dinner jacket.*

HESTER. Bill –

COLLYER. I don't apologize. I've got to see you –

He comes in, glancing at MILLER *as he does so.*

MILLER (*to* HESTER). Yes. That is the most specific advice I can give you. Good night.

He nods to COLLYER *and goes out.* COLLYER *silently hands her an opened letter which he has been holding in his hand.* HESTER *draws in her breath sharply as she sees the handwriting. She reads it through quickly.*

HESTER. When did it arrive?

COLLYER. I don't know. It was found about twenty minutes ago. I gather he dropped it in the box without ringing the bell.

HESTER *re-reads the letter, absently.*

It *is* true, I suppose?

HESTER (*wearily*). Yes. It's true. (*She hands the letter back.*)

COLLYER. When?

HESTER. This afternoon. Just after you'd left.

COLLYER. What was the reason?

HESTER. What happened last night. That's why he was drunk this afternoon. He said we were death to each other –

COLLYER. *In vino veritas.*

HESTER. He wasn't so drunk when he said that.

COLLYER. Then he has more perception than I gave him credit for. What's he going to do?

HESTER. He's taken a job as a test pilot in South America.

COLLYER. I see. (*Glancing at the letter.*) I rather like the phrase: 'Sorry to have caused so much bother.' It has a nice ring of R.A.F. understatement –

He tears the letter up and throws it into the waste-paper basket.

(*After a pause.*) I'm awfully sorry for you, Hester.

HESTER (*her back to him*). That's all right. It was bound to happen one day, I suppose.

COLLYER. I have a faint inkling of how you must be feeling at this moment.

HESTER (*turning. Hard and bright*). Oh, I'll get over it I imagine. You're looking very smart. Where have you been?

COLLYER. At home. I had some people in to dinner.

HESTER. Who?

COLLYER. Olive, the Prestons, an American judge and his wife –

HESTER. Was Olive in good form?

COLLYER. Fairly. She said one very funny thing.

HESTER. What was it?

COLLYER. Damn. I've forgotten. Oh yes. I do remember. Now I come to think of it, it's not all that funny. It must have been the way she said it. She told the American judge he had a face like an angry cupid –

HESTER. An angry cupid? I can just hear her –

She starts to laugh, and then continues longer than the joke appears to warrant.

An angry cupid!

The laugh suddenly turns into sobs. She buries her head in the sofa cushion, desperately but unsuccessfully trying to control her emotion. COLLYER *sits beside her.*

COLLYER. Hester. please. If only I could say something that would help you. (*He strokes her head.*)

HESTER *is succeeding now in recovering herself.*

I know it's small comfort to you at this moment, but this must be for the best. You yourself spoke of an evil affinity, didn't you?

HESTER, *wiping her eyes, does not reply.* COLLYER *looks round the room.*

HESTER. I'm sorry about that. I couldn't help it –

COLLYER. You must get out of this flat as soon as possible. In fact I don't think you should be left alone in it at all.

HESTER. I'll be all right.

COLLYER. I'm not so sure. I think you'd better leave here tonight.

HESTER. Tonight?

COLLYER. You were alone here last night, weren't you?

HESTER. Where could I go?

COLLYER. Well – I could make a very tentative suggestion. In fact the suggestion that Freddie makes in that letter.

HESTER. No, Bill. That's impossible.

COLLYER. Have you forgotten so quickly what I told you this afternoon?

HESTER (*her voice rising*). Stop it, Bill – please –

He is silenced by the note of strain in her voice. She gets up, a little unsteadily, and goes to a cupboard.

I expect you'd like a drink, wouldn't you?

COLLYER. A good idea.

HESTER. Oh dear! I'd forgotten that Freddie had finished the whisky.

COLLYER. It doesn't matter.

HESTER. Wait a moment. Here's something. (*She brings out a bottle of wine.*) Claret. I'm afraid I uncorked it last night. It's from the local grocer. I don't know what your fastidious palate will make of it.

COLLYER. I'm sure it's delicious. (*He opens the bottle.*)

She gives him two glasses. He fills them.

Well? What shall the toast be?

HESTER. The future, I suppose.

COLLYER. May I say our future?

HESTER (*gravely*). No, Bill. Just the future.

They drink in silence.

Is it all right?

COLLYER. Very good. (*After another pause.*) And what's the future to be?

HESTER. I haven't thought yet.

COLLYER. Don't you think you should?

HESTER. I'll stay on here until I can find somewhere else.
I'll try and take a studio if I can – then I'll be able to work
harder. If I can't sell my paintings, I'll get a job –

COLLYER. What sort of job?

HESTER. There must be something I can do.

COLLYER (*quietly*). And you contemplate living alone for the
rest of your life?

HESTER. I don't contemplate anything, Bill. I'm not exactly in
a contemplative mood.

COLLYER. When you are, I'd like you to contemplate a very
different future –

HESTER (*angrily*). Bill, please, I've asked you –

COLLYER (*equally angrily*). Hester, for God's sake, don't you
realize what I'm offering you?

HESTER. And don't *you* realize how difficult it is for me to
refuse?

COLLYER. Then why need you refuse?

HESTER. Because I must. I can't go back to you as your wife,
Bill, because I no longer am your wife. We can't wipe out
this last year as if it had never happened. Don't you understand that?

COLLYER. I only understand that I'm even more in love with
you now than I was on our wedding day.

HESTER (*quietly*). You weren't in love with me on our wedding
day, Bill. You aren't in love with me now, and you never have
been.

COLLYER. Hester!

HESTER. I'm simply a prized possession that has now become
more prized for having been stolen, that's all.

COLLYER (*hurt*). What are you saying?

HESTER (*upset*). You force me to say these things, Bill. Do you think I enjoy hurting you, of all people? Perhaps you'd better go now, and we can talk some other time, when we both feel calmer.

COLLYER. We must talk now. You say I wasn't in love with you when I married you?

HESTER. I know you weren't.

COLLYER. Then why do you suppose I married you? What else did you have to offer me?

HESTER (*interrupting*). I know, Bill, I know. You don't need to remind me of what a bad match I was. I was always very conscious of it. Oh, I'm not denying you married for love – for your idea of love. And so did I – for my idea of love. The trouble seems to be they weren't the same ideas. You see, Bill – I had more to give you – far more – than you ever wanted from me.

COLLYER. How can you say that? You know I wanted your love –

HESTER. No, Bill. You wanted me simply to be a loving wife. There's all the difference in the world.

Pause.

COLLYER. Do you imagine I believed that pathetic story just now about a studio and a job? Do you think I don't know exactly how you visualize your future? (HESTER *is silent.*) You'll never let him go, Hester. You can't. (HESTER *is still silent. Pleadingly.*) Hester, my darling, what you say about me and my feelings for you may be true, but I'm offering you your only chance of life. Why can't you accept? After all, it worked quite happily once.

HESTER. Yes, it did. Very happily.

COLLYER. Well, then?

HESTER *does not reply.* COLLYER *takes her and kisses her. She does not try to prevent him, but responds in no way at all. After a moment he releases her.*

HESTER. You see, Bill, I'm not any longer the same person.

Pause.

You'd better go.

COLLYER *looks away from her and his glance strays round the room.*

(*Impatiently.*) I'll be all right.

COLLYER *nods and goes to the door.*

COLLYER. You still want your divorce then?

HESTER. Yes, Bill. I think it would be best.

COLLYER. There'll be a lot to discuss – business things.

HESTER. Yes. I suppose there will.

COLLYER. For the moment are you all right for money?

HESTER. Please, Bill.

COLLYER. Goodbye, then.

HESTER. Goodbye.

He looks at her puzzled and deeply troubled. He seems to be considering making a final appeal. HESTER turns from his gaze. COLLYER shrugs his shoulders and goes. HESTER, left alone, takes a sip of her wine. She is moving to sit down when the sound of a key in the lock makes her turn sharply. She moves back quickly into the recess formed by the kitchen, out of sight of the front door. This opens furtively to reveal PHILIP WELCH. HESTER comes out of the recess.

HESTER. Freddie?

PHILIP *turns sharply. He seems acutely embarrassed.*

PHILIP. Oh.

HESTER. How did you get in?

PHILIP. It's Page . . . you see, he lent me a key . . . He wanted me to pick up his suitcase. He's got all his washing things in it, apparently, and says he needs them for tonight.

HESTER. Where's he going tonight?

PHILIP (*uncomfortably*). I don't know.

HESTER. Where is he now?

PHILIP. Er – I don't know what the place is called.

HESTER. Where is it?

PHILIP. Somewhere in the West End.

HESTER. Greek Street?

PHILIP (*stubbornly*). I don't know.

Pause.

HESTER. I see. How long have you been with him?

PHILIP. Since nine.

HESTER. And he can do a lot of talking in three hours – especially when he's drunk.

PHILIP. He's not drunk. At least what he says makes sense.

HESTER (*bitterly*). Does it?

PHILIP (*in slightly avuncular tones*). Lady Collyer – may I say something? Page has been very frank with me. Very frank indeed, although I didn't invite his confidence. So I know the whole situation you see, and I do understand what you must be feeling at this moment –

HESTER. Do you, Mr Welch?

PHILIP. I've been in love too, you know. In fact about a year ago I nearly had a bust-up in *my* marriage – over a sort of infatuation I had for a girl – quite the wrong sort of type, really, and it would have been disastrous – but I do know what it means to have to give someone up whom you – think you love. Look – do you think this is awfully impertinent of me?

HESTER. Not at all.

PHILIP (*emboldened*). Well, I do think you ought to – sort of – try and steel yourself to what I'm quite sure is the best course for both of you. Gosh, I know how hard it is, but I do remember, with this girl – she was an actress you know, although she wasn't well-known or anything – I just sat down all alone one day and said to myself – look, on the physical side, she's everything in the world you want. On the other side – what is she? Nothing. So what I did was to write her a letter – and then I went away for a fortnight all by myself – and of course I had hell, but gradually things got sort of clearer in my mind, and when I got back I was out of the wood.

HESTER. I'm so glad. Where was it you went?

PHILIP. Lyme Regis.

HESTER. A very pretty spot. I know it.

PHILIP. Of course I think for you some place like Italy or the South of France would be better.

HESTER. Why better than Lyme Regis?

PHILIP. Well, complete change of atmosphere, you know – nice weather, nobody you know, and lots of time to think things out. And I know if you do think things out honestly, you'll see how awfully petty the whole thing really is – when you get it in perspective. I mean, without trying to be preachy or anything, it *is* really the spiritual values that count in this life, isn't it? I mean the physical side is really awfully unimportant – objectively speaking, don't you think?

HESTER (*gravely*). Objectively speaking. (*She gets up indicating dismissal.*) Well, it's very kind of you, Mr Welch, to give me this advice. I'm very grateful.

PHILIP. Oh, that's all right. I'm glad you didn't fly at me for it. You see Page has been telling me about it all, and I was really awfully interested, because a thing like this it's – well – it throws a sort of light on human nature, really.

HESTER. Yes. I suppose it does.

PHILIP. Well, may I have the bag now, please?

HESTER. It's just through that door.

PHILIP goes into the bedroom, reappearing after a moment with a suitcase.

Where did Freddie tell you to take that bag? To a station or somewhere, or back to the White Angel?

PHILIP. Back to the White – (*He stops abruptly.*)

Pause.

(*Lamely.*) Back to where he is.

HESTER (*quietly*). Would you mind putting the bag down, please, and going?

PHILIP. I'm afraid I can't do that. I promised him I'd bring it to him, you see. Well, goodbye.

He turns towards the door. HESTER is there before him and quickly turns a key in the lock. She removes the key and puts it in her pocket, and she goes towards the telephone, where she turns up a telephone book.

HESTER. I'm sorry for that melodramatic gesture, but I've got to detain you for a moment or two, I'm afraid. (*She begins to dial a telephone number.*) I won't keep you long. There's the remains of a bottle of claret there, if you'd like it.

PHILIP (*stiffly*). No, thank you. (*He goes to the door.*)

HESTER. No, that key won't help you. It's a separate lock.

PHILIP (*angrily*). Look, I really do think –

HESTER. Please sit down. You've got a splendid chance now of resuming your study of human nature.

She is dialling a number. PHILIP stands watching her.

Hullo . . . White Angel? Is Mr Page there? . . . (*Louder.*) Mr Page . . . That's right . . . Oh, he is . . . Mrs Jackson . . . no, Jackson . . . Yes. (*To* PHILIP.) There's a lot of noise in there. (*Pause.*) Hullo? . . . Darling, it's Hester – don't ring off. No scene, I promise . . . I promise, I promise. I only want to know about the job, that's all . . . (*Louder.*) The job . . . Did you see the man? . . . Oh good . . . Oh good . . .

I see. Well done. How soon? . . . As soon as that? . . . Oh, Freddie . . . no, I'm sorry. It was just hearing you say it like that – that's all . . . (*Louder.*) It was just hearing you say it . . . Look, your messenger is here for your bag – only it hasn't got half of what you want for three days. Where are you going to until you leave? . . . No, that's all right. Don't tell me, if you don't want to. I only meant country or town? Now, let's think. You've got your flannels in the bag so you'll just want your tweed coat . . . All right. What did you want done with the rest of your things? . . . Oh, when did you post it? . . . I'll get it tomorrow then . . . The cloakroom at Charing Cross . . . I see . . . Yes. I'll do that . . . Look, Freddie, I want you to do one last thing for me . . . I said I wanted you to do one last thing. Come and collect your bag yourself . . . just to say goodbye, that's all. Surely there's no harm . . . No. I won't, I won't. I promise I won't. I swear to you, on my most sacred word of honour, I won't try and make you stay. I won't even talk, if you don't want me to. You can just take your bag and go . . . I want to see you again, that's all . . . Freddie, trust me, trust me, for pity's sake . . . Freddie, don't ring off – don't –

She looks blankly at the receiver, and then replaces it. She stares at it a moment, evidently wondering whether to dial again, and then decides it would be useless. She goes slowly to the door, puts the key in the lock, and unlocks it, indicating to PHILIP *with a gesture that he is free to go.*

PHILIP (*hesitating*). Didn't you say something about a tweed coat?

HESTER. Did I? Oh yes. It's hanging up on that door.

PHILIP *goes into the bedroom, carrying the suitcase.* HESTER, *left alone, wanders towards the mantelpiece. She looks down at the gas-fire.* PHILIP *reappears with a tweed coat over his arm.*

PHILIP (*on his way to the door*). Well – good night.

HESTER. Good night, Mr Welch. Oh, by the way, your wife is rather worried about you. Perhaps you'd better slip up and see her before you go out again.

PHILIP. Yes. I will. (*Earnestly.*) You're all right alone, aren't you? I mean, you're not going to do anything silly tonight. You must have learnt your lesson from last night.

HESTER. Yes. I've learnt my lesson.

PHILIP. I'm awfully sorry – really I am.

HESTER. Thank you.

PHILIP. I think he ought to have come to fetch his things himself.

HESTER. So do I.

PHILIP. Although of course I understood him not wanting to come round when he thought you might try and stop him, but – still – after you gave him your sacred, solemn word of honour just now –

HESTER *has not previously been looking at* PHILIP. *She now turns slowly to face him.*

HESTER. It might add a little to your appreciation of spiritual values, Mr Welch, if I told you that I hadn't the smallest intention of keeping that sacred, solemn word of honour. If Freddie had come here tonight, I would have made him stay. Of course he knew that perfectly well, and that's why he wouldn't come.

PHILIP, *shocked, stares at her in silence.* HESTER *looks up at him.*

HESTER. You've got exactly the same expression on your face that my father would have had if I'd said that to him. He believed in spiritual values, too, you know – and the pettiness of the physical side.

Pause.

Take the bag to Freddie now. Have you got enough money for a taxi?

PHILIP. Yes, thank you. (*At the door.*) Can I – should I give Page any sort of message from you or anything?

Pause.

HESTER (*quietly*). Just my love.

PHILIP *nods and goes.* HESTER *closes the door after him. After a second of utter stillness she moves quietly to the window, and gently closes it. Then she goes to her bag and searches for a coin. Not finding what she is looking for she turns quickly to the table on to which* FREDDIE *had thrown the shilling. She picks it up and walks to the gas meter, inserts the coin, and we hear it drop. She turns to the front-door and locks it. Then she places a rug carefully on the floor against the door. Turning, she picks up the empty bottle of aspirin, looks at it, and puts it down. Then she pulls from her pocket the sleeping pills given her by* MILLER, *takes a glass from the table, goes into the kitchen, and reappears having filled it with water. Her breath is now coming in short gasps, as if she had been undergoing some strong physical exertion, although her movements until now have not been hurried. There is a knock on the door, arresting her in the action of putting the pills into her mouth.*

(*Impatiently.*) Yes? Who is it?

MILLER (*off*). Miller.

HESTER. What do you want? I'm just going to bed.

MILLER (*off*). I want to see you.

HESTER. Won't it keep to the morning?

MILLER (*off*). No.

HESTER *impatiently goes to the door, pulls the rug up, and throws it on to the sofa where it falls to the floor. She unlocks the door and lets* MILLER *in.*

(*Indicating key.*) Determined not to be disturbed?

HESTER. I usually lock my door at night.

MILLER. It's lucky you didn't last night.

HESTER (*indicating the glass of water*). I was just going to take your pills.

MILLER. So I see.

HESTER. Do you think they're strong enough, Doctor. Could you let me have another two or three in case they don't work?

MILLER, *without replying, picks up the rug from the floor and puts it on the sofa. Then, watched by* HESTER, *he strolls to the gas-fire and with a casual flick of his foot, kicks on the tap. We hear the hiss of escaping gas. He kicks it off.*

I said could you let me have –

MILLER. I heard you. The answer is no.

HESTER. Why not?

MILLER. I've been involved enough with the police. I don't want to be accused now of giving drugs to a suicidal patient. (*He holds out his hand.*)

HESTER. Aren't you letting your imagination run away with you, Doctor?

MILLER. No. I want those pills back, please.

HESTER. Why?

MILLER. If you put a rug down in front of a door it's wiser to do it when the lights are out.

HESTER (*hysterically*). Why are you spying on me? Why can't you leave me alone?

MILLER. I'm not trying to decide for you whether you live or die. That choice is yours and you have quite enough courage to make it for yourself –

HESTER (*with a despairing cry*). Courage!

MILLER. Oh yes. It takes courage to condemn yourself to death. Most suicides die to escape. *You're* dying because you feel unworthy to live. Isn't that true?

HESTER (*wildly*). How do I know what's true? I only know that after tonight I won't be able to face life any more.

MILLER. What is there so hard about facing life? Most people seem to be able to manage it.

HESTER. How can anyone live without hope?

MILLER. Quite easily. To live without hope can mean to live without despair.

HESTER. Those are just words.

MILLER. Words can help you if your mind can only grasp them. (*He twists her roughly round to face him. Harshly.*) Your Freddie has left you. He's never going to come back again. Never in the world. Never.

At each word she wilts as if at a physical blow.

HESTER (*wildly*). I know. I know. That's what I can't face.

MILLER (*with brutal force*). Yes, you can. That word 'never'. Face that and you can face life. Get beyond hope. It's your only chance.

HESTER. What is there beyond hope?

MILLER. Life. You must believe that. It's true – I know.

HESTER*'s storm of tears is subsiding. She raises her head to look at him.*

HESTER (*at length*). You can still find some purpose in living.

MILLER. What purpose?

HESTER. You have your work at the hospital.

MILLER. For me the only purpose in life is to live it. My work at the hospital is a help to me in that. That is all. If you looked perhaps you might also find some help for yourself.

HESTER. What help?

MILLER. Haven't you got your work too? (*He makes a gesture towards the paintings.*)

HESTER. Oh that. (*Wearily.*) There's no escape for me through that.

MILLER. Not through that, or that. (*With a wide gesture he indicates the later paintings.*) But perhaps through that. (*He points to the early painting.*) I'm not an art expert, but

I believe there was talent here. Just a spark, that's all, which with a little feeding, might have become a little flame. Not a great fire, which could have illumined the world – oh no – I'm not saying that. But the world is a dark enough place for even a little flicker to be welcome.

He hands her a glass of water, which she drinks. Then he turns back to the picture.

I'd like to buy that.

HESTER *gazes at the picture listlessly for a moment. Then she gets up wearily, goes to the picture, and hands it to him. He smiles.*

How much?

HESTER. It's a gift.

MILLER *shakes his head, still smiling. He pulls out his wallet and removes two pound notes.* HESTER *shakes her head.* MILLER *puts the notes on the table.*

MILLER. Look. I'm going to put these notes down here. It's what I can afford to give you – not what I think the picture's worth. If you're determined not to sell it, slip the notes into an envelope and address them to me. I shall understand, and be sorry. Good night.

HESTER. Good night, Doctor.

MILLER (*turning*). Not Doctor, please.

Pause.

HESTER. Good night, my friend.

MILLER. I could wish that you meant that.

HESTER (*quietly*). What makes you so sure that I don't mean it?

MILLER (*also quietly*). I hope that I may be given a proof that you do – by tomorrow morning.

HESTER. Are you asking me to make my choice in order to help you?

MILLER (*smiling*). Surely I have a right to feel sad if I lose a new-found friend – especially one whom I so much like and respect.

HESTER (*bitterly*). Respect?

MILLER. Yes, respect.

HESTER. Please, don't be too kind to me.

He approaches her quickly and takes her shoulders.

MILLER. Listen to me. To see yourself as the world sees you may be very brave, but it can also be very foolish. Why should you accept the world's view of you as a weak-willed neurotic – better dead than alive? What right have they to judge? To judge you they must have the capacity to feel as you feel. And who has? One in a thousand. You alone know how you have felt. And you alone know how unequal the battle has always been that your will has had to fight.

HESTER. 'I tried to be good and failed.' Isn't that the excuse that all criminals make?

MILLER. When they make it justly, it's a just excuse.

HESTER. Does it let them escape the sentence?

MILLER. Yes, if the judge is fair – and not blind with hatred for the criminal – as you are for yourself.

HESTER. If you could find me one extenuating circumstance – one single reason why I should respect myself – even a little.

The door is abruptly thrown open and FREDDIE *appears on the threshold.*

FREDDIE. Hullo.

HESTER. Hullo.

Pause.

MILLER (*to* HESTER). You must find that reason for yourself.

He touches her hand, nods to FREDDIE, *and goes.*

FREDDIE. Did I interrupt something?

HESTER. No. Not really.

FREDDIE. He seems quite a good bloke, old Miller.

HESTER. Yes. He does. Did you come for your bag?

FREDDIE. Yes.

HESTER. That boy took it with him.

FREDDIE. Oh. Well, he'll leave it at the Angel. I'll get it all right.

HESTER. Come in, Freddie. Don't stand in the door.

FREDDIE *shuffles in.*

How are you feeling now?

FREDDIE. All right.

HESTER. Thank you for coming.

FREDDIE. I shouldn't have sent the kid anyway, I suppose.

HESTER. Had any food?

FREDDIE. Yes. I had a bite at the Belvedere. What about you?

HESTER. Oh, I'll get myself something later.

There is a pause, while FREDDIE *still watches her apprehensively.*

When exactly are you off to Rio?

FREDDIE. Thursday. I told you.

HESTER. Oh yes, of course. By boat?

FREDDIE. Oh no. Flying.

HESTER. Oh yes, of course. By the Azores, isn't it?

FREDDIE. No. London, West Africa – then across to Natal.

HESTER. Sounds exciting.

FREDDIE. Oh, I don't know. Oh, by the way – about the rent. My golf clubs will fetch thirty or forty quid. They'll take care of old Ma Elton and a few odd bills.

HESTER. Won't you need them?

FREDDIE. No. I can't fly them.

HESTER. I'll pack the rest of your things tonight and get them round to Charing Cross in the morning.

FREDDIE. No hurry.

Pause.

What are you going to do, Hes?

HESTER. I'm not quite sure yet, Freddie. I think I'll stay on here for a bit.

FREDDIE. I dropped a note in at Bill's house. He'll probably be round.

HESTER. He's been round.

FREDDIE. Oh. Are you – ?

HESTER. No.

FREDDIE. I'm sorry.

HESTER. It's all right. It wouldn't have worked.

FREDDIE. No. I suppose not. I didn't know. You'll go on with your painting, will you?

HESTER. Yes. I think so. As a matter of fact I might even go to an Art School, and start from the beginning again.

FREDDIE. Good idea. It's never too late to begin again. Isn't that what they say?

HESTER. Yes. They do.

There is a long pause. FREDDIE *seems to be waiting for* HESTER *to say something, but she stands quite still, looking at him.*

FREDDIE (*at length*). Well –

HESTER (*in a clear, calm voice*). Goodbye, Freddie.

Pause.

FREDDIE (*murmuring*). Goodbye, Hes.

*He moves to the door. HESTER still does not move.
FREDDIE turns, waiting for her to say something. She
does not. He suddenly walks up to her.*

Thank you for everything.

HESTER. Thank you, too.

*He kisses her. She accepts the embrace without in any way
returning it.*

FREDDIE. I'm going to miss you, Hes.

*After a moment, FREDDIE releases her, goes to the door,
and turns round, still with a faint air of bewildered appeal.*

HESTER (*loudly and clearly*). Goodbye.

*FREDDIE stares at her, turns, and shuffles out, closing the
door. HESTER stands rigid, her face utterly expressionless.
Then she moves quickly across the room and reaches up for a
suitcase which is on a shelf above the bedroom door. She
puts the suitcase – which is labelled F. T. PAGE – on a chair,
and goes across to collect those clothes of FREDDIE's that
are hanging on the pegs by the front-door. As she begins to
take these down, methodically, one by one, she appears
momentarily to lose her hard composure. She buries her face
in his mackintosh, and remains so for a few brief seconds.
Then she roughly pulls the mackintosh down from the hook
and throws it and the other clothes on to the sofa.*

*The light seems to hurt her eyes. She turns out all but a
reading lamp. Then she goes to the fire, turns on the gas, and
lights it with a match. She stands by the fire for a moment,
watching the flame change from orange to red. She has
turned back to the sofa, and is quietly folding one of
FREDDIE's scarves as the curtain falls.*

The End.

**Other titles by the same author
published by Nick Hern Books**

After the Dance

The Browning Version and *Harlequinade*

Cause Célèbre

First Episode

Flare Path

French Without Tears

In Praise of Love

Love in Idleness / Less Than Kind

Rattigan's Nijinsky
    (adapted from Rattigan's screenplay by Nicholas Wright)

Separate Tables

Who is Sylvia? and *Duologue*

The Winslow Boy